PURE & HEALTHY

ISBN: 978-81-942068-1-1

Roli Books 2019
Published in India by Roli Books
M-75, Greater Kailash II Market,
New Delhi – 110 048, India.
Phone: +91-11-4068 2000
Email: info@rolibooks.com
Website: www.rolibooks.com

Design: Pallavi Agarwala
Pre-press: Jyoti Dey
Production: Lavinia Rao

Printed and bound in Nutech Print Services

PURE & HEALTHY

HEALTHY INDIAN VEGETARIAN CUISINE

VIDHU MITTAL

Nutritionist
RADHIKA KARLE

Photographs
SANJAY RAMCHANDRAN

Lustre Press
Roli Books

CONTENTS

For every lover of healthy vegetarian food

INTRODUCTION

Food and nutrition form a vital part of our overall well-being. The idea for this book first took shape when I was diagnosed with gluten allergy and began trying out new gluten-free dishes that were appetizing without compromising on taste. I soon realized that there are many who are interested in similarly easy recipes that can cater to specific nutritional requirements for diabetes, weight management, heart problems, etc., as well as for those who just want to eat healthy. The aim of this book is to get you back to your kitchens to create truly healthy food that nourishes you, inside and out, without making compromises and taking away the joy of eating.

Healthy food nourishes mind and body, helps boost immunity and provides energy to perform everyday tasks. My research for balanced and wholesome diets led me to explore traditional vegetables and ingredients like millets, sorghum and ragi – all packed with vital nutrients and minerals, offering several health benefits. Over the years, these traditional ingredients have disappeared from our kitchens; rediscovering them has filled my food journey with a renewed sense of excitement and joy. My focus has since been to make use of these natural, fresh, healthy and preservative-free ingredients that are nutritious and wholesome. A variety of these ingredients are easily available, and have been innovatively combined in the book to make delicious and visually appealing dishes by accentuating colour and natural flavour, breaking the myths of healthy food being bland, insipid and uninspiring.

Radhika Karle, a well-known nutritionist, helped me establish the right proportions of all ingredients by balancing each dish with the appropriate nutrients and calories. She has done nutritional analyses and calorie counts for each recipe. We have also drawn out interesting meal plans that are suitable to general well-being and can also cater to specific dietary needs. These plans specify suitable portions size and provide a balance of carbohydrates, proteins and fats.

As with my previous books, simplicity remains the very essence of all recipes – each recipe has easy-to-understand steps supported by stepwise photographs, followed by useful hints and tips. I hope you find in this book the subtle flavours and varying textures of homely Indian food, and take part in a joyful rediscovery of our healthy food roots.

I have always found cooking to be not only therapeutic but also helpful in knitting the family together with lots of love and affection. Nothing brings people together like food does; I strongly recommend that each one of us cooks at least one meal for the family ourselves, and relish its therapeutic benefits by enjoying the process.

I hope you and your loved ones enjoy trying out these recipes as much as I have enjoyed bringing these simple, pure and healthy recipes together for you.

Vidhu Mittal

ACKNOWLEDGEMENTS

A cookbook is a collective effort with contributions from many. I would like to thank those who helped make it happen.

Abhishek Poddar was a motivator, who helped with the creative design, aesthetics and vision of the book.

Radhika Karle, whose tireless efforts, invaluable inputs and deep knowledge of nutritional value made this book possible. She has been an amazing partner full of ideas, and accepts no compromise.

Sanjay Ramchandran, whose endless patience and passion for perfection helped bring out the true essence of each recipe through exquisite photographs; his love for food helps.

Jagdish Babu DK systematically and patiently sorted thousands of photographs, and helped select and reorganize them diligently.

Priya and **Nasreen** helped type the recipes from just outlines to final draft stages; their days of hard work are reflected in this book.

Team at Roli, for putting together the design, careful editing, compilation and final production.

And most importantly, my husband **Som**, our children **Nidhi, Tarang** and **Siddharth** and our domestic help, **Jasmine**, who helped and supported me through my journey of this book.

Our two grandchildren, **Sudha** and **Amitdeep**, were my constant critics as they tried out these new dishes. Their approval was the ultimate test.

BEING HEALTHY
Suggestions from the Expert

*P*ure & *Healthy* focuses on clean and nutritious eating with fresh ingredients. Natural ingredients that were regularly consumed by our forefathers, but which have reduced in popularity over time, are therefore an important part of the recipes. Ghee, a fat that greatly aids in the absorption of fat-soluble vitamins (vitamins A, D, E and K) as well as in digestion, has been added to the book. Rice bran oil is also back on the shelf for its proportionate amount of monounsaturated and polyunsaturated fats, both of which are heart-healthy. And when it comes to desserts, the idea was not to recommend unhealthy dishes but to provide recipes for more wholesome options.

For a truly successful weight management plan, then, one must not and need not starve oneself. Instead, it is important to understand the number of calories and the distribution of macronutrients – carbohydrates, protein and fat – in your meal plan. The number of servings of each of the food groups (starch, fruit, vegetables, beans/legumes and fat) can be determined from here and then distributed throughout the day. To this end, each recipe in the book has a recommended portion per serving, and is measured in a standardized way with measuring teaspoons (1 tsp = 5 ml), tablespoons (1 Tbsp =15 ml) and measuring cups (1 cup = 200 ml). Dry measurements will differ in weight due to their volume and texture.

Pure & Healthy encourages simple and effective lifestyle improvements that can bring about positive body composition changes. Along with the recipes this book has to offer, here are some tips to help you begin your wellness journey:

- Eat fresh, seasonal and local foods. Avoid processed and packaged foods.
- Drinking a minimum of two litres of water per day is a good place to start. Water plays a major role in regulating body temperature, transporting water-soluble vitamins and aiding in digestion.
- Avoid excess amounts of tea and coffee as they further dehydrate the body.
- Exercise every day for 30–45 minutes at a moderate to high intensity. Include a combination of cardiovascular exercise, resistance training and stretching in your weekly exercise routine.
- Keep a check on your vitamin D3 and vitamin B12 levels. Vitamin D3 plays a major role in converting calcium into a form that the body can absorb, therefore ensuring bones stay strong. Vitamin B12 helps convert food to energy that the cells of the body can then absorb and utilize.
- The most important part of your wellness journey will be your rest and recovery time as this is truly what is going to ensure you see results. 7–8 hours of consecutive, undisturbed sleep are of utmost importance to allow the body to recover from exercise and to build lean body mass.

Supported by my learnings at the Yogendra Institute in Mumbai, India and my master's degree in Nutrition and Dietetics from Texas Woman's University, Houston, I have worked with Vidhu to bring together ancient Ayurvedic practices with nutritional sciences to the pages of *Pure & Healthy*.

So try a recipe at the next party you host, and see how pleasantly surprised your guests will be when they hear it is filled with pure and healthy ingredients!

Be and remain healthy,
Radhika Karle

KNOW YOUR FRUITS & DRIED FRUITS

Apple (*seb*): This fruit comes in different varieties and colours. The skin colour varies from green to pink to bright red. Below the skin, there is off-white, crispy, juicy pulp. It is used in salads, drinks, desserts, etc. Apples are rich in dietary fibre and help in the digestive process.

Avocado (*makhan fal*): This pear-shaped fruit has uneven green skin with yellowish-green flesh inside. The skin and the big seed inside are discarded. Avocado flesh is used in salads, to make guacamole and is relished on breads. It is rich in fibre and heart-healthy fatty acids.

Banana (*kela*): This fruit is generally elongated and curved with soft flesh inside. The peel colour varies from green to yellow, to brown when ripe. It is used in smoothies and desserts. Banana is rich in potassium and high in dietary fibre, which makes you feel fuller for longer.

Kiwi fruit: This is an oblong berry with downy, brownish-green skin. It has vibrant deep green flesh with small and crunchy edible black seeds. Kiwi fruit is often used in salads, drinks, desserts, etc. It is a rich source of vitamin A, vitamin C, dietary fibre and antioxidants.

Mango (*aam*): It is the king of fruits. Both ripe and raw mangoes are used. The raw mango has green skin and white flesh that is sour in taste. The ripe mango's skin colour varies from green to yellow, and has orange flesh and non-edible seed inside. It helps to purify the blood and is rich in antioxidants.

Orange (*santra*): This fruit is covered with thick green to yellow skin. The orange inside is divided into pulpy, juicy segments. It is used to make drinks, salads and desserts, and in some vegetable preparations. It is a rich source of vitamin C and acts as an antioxidant.

Papaya (*papita*): This fruit is oval in shape, and both the raw and the ripe fruit are relished. Raw papaya is made into salads and curries, whereas the ripe variety is used as a table fruit. It is rich in antioxidants and is anti-inflammatory. It treats constipation and improves digestion.

Pomelo (*chakotra*): This fruit is large with a light green or yellow rind, usually one inch-thick. Pomelo fruit segments can be yellow or pink in colour. The fruit has a tangy taste. It is used to make drinks and salads. This fruit improves digestion and contains potassium, vitamin C and dietary fibre.

Star Fruit (*kamrak*): This yellowish-green fruit has five wings, edible skin and thick flesh. It has a waxy coat. It can be enjoyed as a fruit, pickled or as a jam. It is rich in dietary fibre, vitamin C, B vitamins and antioxidants.

Strawberry: This cone-shaped fruit belongs to the rose family and comes in various sizes. Its colour ranges from pale orange to bright red, and its flavour from sweet to tart. Strawberries have a short shelf life. They can be relished in drinks, desserts, preserves, etc. They are packed with vitamins, fibre and antioxidants.

Watermelon (*tarbooj*): This oblong fruit is green in colour, sometimes with white bands running from end to end. Watermelon is a popular summer fruit – sweet and crunchy, it is 91 per cent water. It is used in drinks and salads. It is rich in antioxidants and vitamin C.

Almonds (*badam*): This nut is highly nutritious, usually eaten raw and also made into a beverage (almond milk). Slivered almonds are used as a garnish on Indian desserts and salads. It is rich in protein, vitamin E and dietary fibre, keeping the heart healthy and lowering cholesterol.

 Amaranth seeds (*ramdana*): These seeds are procured from the Amaranth plant. They are tiny, round seeds that are a pale, white colour. Roasted, popped amaranth seeds are used in Indian desserts. They are rich in antioxidants, dietary fibre and vitamin C.

 Black raisins (*kali kishmish*): Raisins are dried black grapes. They are used in certain Indian desserts. They are high in fibre, and their rich iron content makes them a natural blood purifier when it comes to treating anaemia.

 Dates (*khajoor*): A dried fruit that comes from the date palm tree. Dates have a honey sweetness and are enjoyed both ripe and semi-dried. They are a delicious addition to dips, chutneys and desserts. They are a rich source of protein and iron.

 Figs (*anjeer*): They are pear-shaped fruits available in dried form. They are sweet to taste and filled with natural fibre. Figs are used to make salads, sweeteners, jams and ice-creams. They are rich in iron and high in fibre.

 Flax seeds (*alsi ke beej*): Also known as linseeds, they comes in two different colours: brown and yellow. Flax seeds are tiny, nutty-flavoured seeds. For better absorption and digestion, grind them before use. They are high in dietary fibre and help to lower cholesterol.

 Fox nuts (*makhana*): Also known as gorgon nuts, fox nuts are the seeds of the flowering plant that belongs to the water lily family. Fox nuts are white with a few dark spots. They are used to make sweets and savoury Indian delicacies. Fox nuts are rich in antioxidants and magnesium.

 Pine nuts (*chilgoza*): Ivory-coloured and slender, pine nuts have a thin, soft brown shell and are often toasted to accentuate their natural nutty flavour. The unique crunch and flavour of pine nuts are used to enhance salads, vegetable preparations, desserts, etc. They are rich in protein, iron and monounsaturated fats.

 Pistachios (*pista*): Pale green and encased in a hard beige shell. Pistachios can be used whole, chopped or slivered as a garnish. They are packed with dietary fibre and vitamins A and E.

 Pumpkin seeds (*kaddu ke beej*): These seeds are hulled and roasted before use. They are olive green inside and have a sweet, nutty flavour. Pumpkin seeds are enjoyed as a crunchy dressing on salads. They are rich in antioxidants, iron and dietary fibre.

 Sunflower seeds (*surajmukhi ke beej*): These seeds are dehulled kernels from their shells. They can be used for garnishing on soups and salads or as a mid-time snack. Sunflower seeds are rich in antioxidants and proteins.

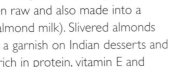

WELCOMING LENTILS & MILLETS

The edible seeds of peas and beans are known as lentils but are also referred to as 'pulses'. They are often paired with rice and Indian breads as well as added to salads and soups. A variety of lentils exist with colours that range from yellow to red, orange to green, brown to black. Lentils are sold in many forms: with or without the skin, whole or split. They contain high levels of protein, vitamin B1, dietary fibre and minerals.

De-husked, split Bengal gram, roasted
(bhuni chana dal)

Red kidney beans
(rajmah)

Black chickpea
(kala chana)

Skinned, split green gram
(dhuli moong dal)

Black-eyed peas
(lobhia dal)

Split green gram
(chilka moong dal)

Butter beans
(vaal)

Whole green gram
(sabut moong dal)

De-husked, split black gram
(dhuli urad dal)

Whole red lentil
(kale masoor)

De-husked, split Bengal gram
(chana dal)

Yellow lentil
(arhar dal)

Moth bean
(moth)

Millets have been an important staple food in Indian history. Millet grains are a repository of protein, fibre, vitamins and minerals. Either they are used whole in Indian preparations or made into flour. Since the flour texture is coarse, it requires patience to make them into dough and, later, when rolling and cooking them into a bread. The higher nutritional value of a cooked millet dish keeps you full for a longer time. Millets are the most versatile ingredient, and are used to prepare idlis, dosas, khichdi, etc.

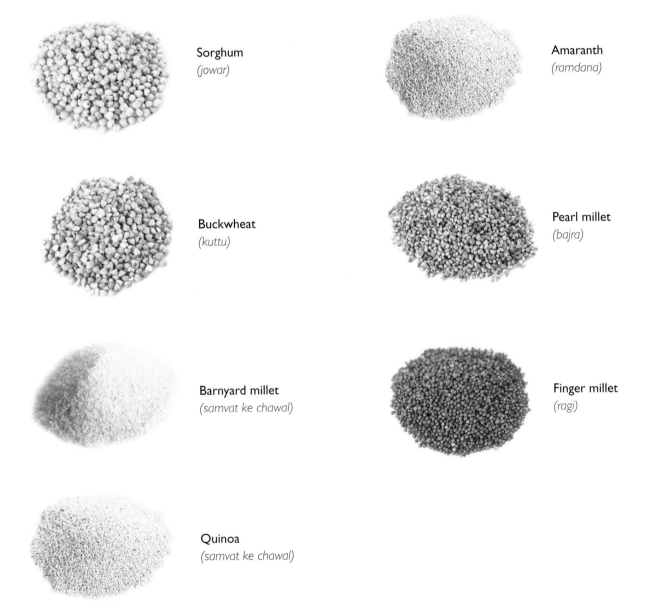

Sorghum
(jowar)

Amaranth
(ramdana)

Buckwheat
(kuttu)

Pearl millet
(bajra)

Barnyard millet
(samvat ke chawal)

Finger millet
(ragi)

Quinoa
(samvat ke chawal)

DISCOVER SPICES

Spices are indispensable additions that enhance the flavour, aroma and colour of a dish. They may be used whole, powdered, in their natural form or after sun drying. The real flavour of a spice is enhanced when it is either first roasted or pre-heated in a cooking medium or when added directly during the cooking process.

Asafoetida (*hing*): This spice has a strong odour and flavour and is obtained from the resin of a plant. The resin is traditionally powdered by using mortar and pestle. Usually just a pinch is added as it can infuse the entire dish. Asafoetida aids in digestion and also reduces flatulence. It is rich in antioxidants.

Bay leaf (*tej patta*): An aromatic herb. Usually 2–3 leaves are gently heated in oil before the addition of other ingredients so that their subtle, fragrant aroma and flavour infuse the entire dish. The are used to season certain pilafs, soups and curries. Bay leaves are inedible and usually removed before serving. They help in digestion and are rich in antioxidants.

Black cardamom (*badi elaichi*): This robust and highly aromatic spice is a dark brown pod with tough and wrinkly skin, used whole or crushed. It exudes a smoky, camphor-like flavour when cooked. It is used in soups, rice and lentils, and is also a key ingredient of the Indian spice mix (*garam masala*). It helps in respiratory problems and act as an antioxidant.

Black peppercorn (*sabut kali mirch*): This is a sun-dried berry of a pepper plant. It can be used whole or freshly ground and adds an increasing pungency to a variety of dishes including soups and salads. Black peppercorn is rich in magnesium, calcium, iron and potassium.

Carom seeds (*ajwain*): These are small, pale, khaki-brown seeds that are highly aromatic with a slightly pungent flavour. Usually used whole, just a little added to the seasoning is enough to flavour the entire dish. Carom seeds aid in digestion and have anti-bacterial and anti-fungal qualities.

Cinnamon (*dalchini*): This aromatic spice is from the inner bark of a tree, and is sold as quills, sticks and in powdered form. The whole bark of cinnamon retains its flavour forever. It has a woody aroma and a warm, bitter-sweet flavour. It is rich in antioxidants and controls blood sugar levels.

Clove (*laung*): Dark brown in colour, cloves look like small nails and are dried flower buds that are highly aromatic and have a sharp tingly flavour. Almost always used whole and in moderation, they are added to flavour both sweet and savoury dishes. Cloves are used in the preparation of Indian spice mix (*garam masala*). It is rich in antioxidants and vitamin C.

Coriander seeds (*dhaniya*): These greenish-brown seeds are the dried fruit of the coriander plant. The seeds have an earthy, nutty aroma and a mildly savoury flavour. Coriander seeds in all forms are rich in dietary fibre, lower blood sugar and improve cholesterol levels.

Cumin seeds (*jeera*): These are small, elongated seeds that have a distinctly warm and slightly bitter flavour when raw. Cumin seeds emit their own earthy flavour after being gently sautéed in oil. They can also be roasted, ground and dusted on yoghurt dishes like *raitas*. They are rich in iron and copper.

Fennel seeds (*saunf*): These are small, elongated, light-green seeds that have a sweet and refreshing flavour. Fennel seeds are used whole and in powdered form. The whole seeds are used to season the dish, and are also eaten after meals as they can act as a mouth freshener. They are rich in dietary fibre, help in digestion and control acidity.

Fenugreek seeds (*methi dana*): These seeds are hard, roughly angular and pale yellow in colour. A small amount of fenugreek seeds lends its bitter flavour when used as seasoning. It is a good source of vitamin A, calcium and dietary fibre.

Green cardamom (*choti elaichi*): This spice has a thin green outer shell with tiny black seeds inside. It is highly aromatic, and its seeds are crushed to flavour desserts and curries, lending a sweet flavour and distinctively refreshing aroma. It is a rich source of vitamin C, calcium and magnesium.

Kokum: It is a dried fruit. For usage, semi-dried kokum is soaked in water and sieved to extract the pulp. When added to food, it lends a purple colour and a sour taste. Kokum is used in lentils, curries and drinks. It is rich in antioxidants and vitamin C.

Mango powder (*amchur*): Raw, sour, green mangoes are sun-dried and powdered to produce this fine beige powder with a slightly fibrous texture. It has a warm tanginess. A small quantity is usually added to vegetable dishes towards the end of the cooking process. It improves digestion and is rich in vitamins A and E.

Mustard seeds: These are small round seeds from the mustard plant and comes in three colours: black (*rai*), brown and yellow (*sarson*). The seeds are used for the initial seasoning of the dish. Mustard powder is used in certain pickles to lend a tangy and sour flavour. It is a good source of omega-3 fatty acids, dietary fibre and iron.

Red chilli (*lal mirch*) **powder:** It is a hot spice prepared from ground red chillies and is added to most Indian dishes. The heat depends on the variety of red chilli used. Kashmiri red chillies are comparatively less spicy. It contains sufficient amounts of vitamins A and C.

Star anise (*chakra phool*): It is a dried, star-shaped spice with eight segments. Star anise has a mild woody flavour and is dark brown in colour. It is used to spice soups, pilafs and curries. It is rich in antioxidants.

Turmeric (*haldi*) **powder:** Turmeric is an underground stem, and its powder is used to enhance flavour in most Indian vegetable preparations. It is bright yellow in colour and imparts an earthy aroma and a slightly bitter flavour to foods. It is rich in antioxidants and contains anti-inflammatory properties.

GOODNESS OF VEGETABLES

LEAFY GREENS

 Arugula/Rocket lettuce: Fresh green in colour with delightfully pungent leaves. Arugula provides high levels of protein, thiamine, riboflavin, vitamin B6, zinc and copper. It is ideal for raising good cholesterol levels and lowering the bad in your system.

 Basil: Also known as Thai or sweet basil. The leaves of this sweet herb are lush green, with a warm clove-like flavour and heady aroma. They may be added to flavour drinks, soups and salads. It is rich in vitamin K, calcium and iron.

 Bok Choy: It is also known as Chinese cabbage. The leaves are smooth and dark green in colour. Bok Choy is eaten raw in salads or sautéed in oil until it is translucent. It is a rich source of vitamins A and K.

 **Celery:** With firm, light green stalks and ribbed, dark green leaves, celery stalk has a juicy, crunchy texture and a mildly herbal aftertaste. Usually, the stalks are enjoyed in crudites, drinks, salads and soups while the leaves are used as garnish. Celery is rich in vitamins and minerals.

 Coriander/Cilantro (*dhaniya*): Fresh coriander ranges in colour from light to dark green and has long stems. The tender stem and leaves are fragrant and have a refreshing flavour, best enjoyed fresh in Indian homes when preparing chutneys or as a garnish. It is good as an antibiotic to overcome digestive problems such as diarrhoea. A nutritional power house, coriander is a good source of thiamine, zinc and vitamin A.

 Curry leaves (*kadhipatta*): These are the shiny green leaves of the curry leaf tree. They are usually added as part of the initial seasoning so that their strong aroma and unique flavour infuse the entire dish. They are rich in vitamins and minerals.

 **Goosefoot leaves** (*bathua*): These leaves are dark with uneven, jagged edges and have warming properties. They have an earthy flavour that is enhanced by steaming. Goosefoot leaves are rich in vitamins K and A.

 Iceberg lettuce: This lettuce, when fresh, will have crisp leaves that show no signs of wilting. Iceberg lettuce has a low calorie content. This vegetable contains a considerable amount of folate, a mineral that is essential for preventing birth defects, and is rich in vitamins A, K and C.

 **Lemongrass:** This is a coarse and tufted plant with linear leaves and is utilized for its distinct lemon flavour and citrusy aroma. The chopped grass can be bruised to release its flavour. Lemongrass tea has sedative properties and is also beneficial for treating constipation, nausea and stomach aches. It is rich in vitamin A and iron.

 Mint (*pudina*): This aromatic herb with intense green leaves and purple-tinged stems has a mild, peppery flavor. Mint is used extensively to make condiments including chutneys and dips, as well as in vegetable and rice preparations. It is rich in antioxidants.

Mustard leaves: Available only in winter months in India, its leaves are crispy and peppery in taste. Mustard leaves can be sautéed in oil or made into the famous Sarso Ka Saag. They help in treating colds and arthritis. The top of the leaves possess higher amounts of vitamin K and A, as well as antioxidants.

Parsley: This lush green herb is available in two varieties: curly leaves and flat leaves. In India, parsley is often mistaken for cilantro, but parsley leaves have a distinctively fresh, slightly peppery flavour. It is used to flavour soups and salads, and is rich in dietary fibre.

Red Amaranth: The colour of its leaves ranges from purple to red to green. The entire vegetable, including stem and leaves, is generally stir-fried in oil. It is loaded with iron, vitamins, essential minerals and dietary fibre.

Romaine lettuce: This dark green lettuce is full of nutrients and low in calories. Mainly used for salads and garnishings, it has the ability to improve heart health. Romaine lettuce is also a good source of vitamins A and K, and plays a big role in bone metabolism.

Spinach (*palak*): These crisp dark leaves have a robust, earthy flavour and a slightly bitter aftertaste. Young leaves are often used in salads. Spinach may be steamed or sautéed and then added to vegetable or lentil dishes. They are a rich source of vitamin K.

Spring Onion (*hara pyaz*): Also known as scallions or salad onions, they have long, green, edible stalks and small white bulbs. They are milder in flavour than regular onions and are added to salads, soups, rice and vegetable preparations. They are rich in vitamins A and K.

Tropicana green leaf lettuce: This lush green leaf with a crinkled top has a mildly bitter-sweet aftertaste. Used mainly in salads and sandwiches, this lettuce is a rich source of vitamins K and A.

GREEN VEGETABLES

Bitter gourd (*karela*): This gourd's colour varies from light to dark green. It has rough but watery skin. Regular consumption of bitter gourd juice improves stamina. Also known as bitter melon, it is power-packed with beneficial antioxidants and vitamins.

Bottle gourd (*lauki*): This light green vegetable can vary in size, shape and length, but broadly has slightly hairy skin and soft, white, edible seeds. It is also known as Calabash. It is rich in fibre and therefore aids in digestion. Bottle gourd is low in calories and contains small amounts of vitamin C, calcium, iron and zinc.

Broccoli: It has glossy, deep green leaves with long, thick stems, and is one of the best cruciferous vegetables. Its flowering green head is eaten as a vegetable. Broccoli is enjoyed in soups, salads and vegetable preparations. Steaming of the broccoli helps in better retention of vitamin C. It is full of dietary fibre.

Cluster beans (*guar phalli*): These beans are double ridged and light green in colour, with removable strings on both sides and edible soft seeds. It is a low-calorie vegetable, yet a power house of nutrition with proteins, minerals, vitamins and dietary fibre.

Cucumber (*khira*): This long, cylindrical vegetable can vary in colours, from green to white. Cucumbers are found both large and small and are a perfect blend of fibre and water. The skin contains high levels of vitamin A. They can be used in salads, drinks and yoghurt preparations.

Drumstick (*sahjanki phalli*): This long, slender vegetable is green in colour and has smooth, ribbed skin and edible triangular seed-pods. They can be cut into desired sizes to remove its strings from all sides, and parboiled to make into soups, sambhar and curries. Drumsticks are a rich source of vitamin C and dietary minerals.

Flat green beans (*sem*): These are light to dark green in colour with a flat surface and contain edible beans inside. The young beans are stringless. They are used to make soups, rice and vegetable preparations. These flat beans are rich in protein, fibre, vitamins and minerals. It is a heart-healthy vegetable.

Gooseberry (*amla*): This vegetable is round, firm, light green, ribbed and translucent with an inedible seed inside. It is very sour and has a bitter aftertaste. Gooseberry is traditionally used in India to make ayurvedic medicines and is frequently used in drinks and pickles. It is a good source of vitamin C.

Green banana (*kacha kela*): Also known as Plantain and 'raw banana', it has smooth and thick green skin with starchy flesh inside. They are less sweet than regular bananas. Green bananas are used in kebabs, soups, stews and other vegetable preparations. They are rich in dietary fibre and vitamins A and C.

Green chickpeas: Commonly known as young garbanzo beans, they are plucked while immature in their green state to retain their natural colour and moisture. They are to be eaten fresh in salads, and partially steamed to make vegetable preparations. They are a good source of iron, calcium and vitamins A and C.

Green chilli (*hari mirch*): This is a fiery little vegetable with shiny and smooth green skin. It is available in many varieties that differ in shape, size and pungency, but all add a spicy taste to food. Biting into a raw green chilli increases metabolism and is good for arthritis. It is a great source of vitamins A and C.

Green peas (*hara mattar*): Its fresh peas come nestled within bright, glossy green pods and are mildly sweet. Peas can be steamed, while tender ones can be sautéed and made into vegetable preparations. They are a good source of protein, vitamin C, iron, copper and manganese.

Haricot beans: These pleasantly green beans are stringless and have smooth skin. Haricot beans need a minimal necessary cooking duration to retain their nutrients. These beans can be added to soups, salads, rice and vegetable preparations. They are a good source of magnesium, protein, thiamine, vitamin C and dietary fibre.

Indian baby pumpkin (*tinda*): Also known as apple gourd, this vegetable has light green, slightly hairy skin with white flesh and edible seeds. It has a subtle flavour. This vegetable is 94 per cent water and hence helps in digestion by relieving stomach acidity. It is a rich source of vitamins A and C.

Long green beans (*lobhia phalli*): Also known as yard long beans, they are uniformly light green in colour with edible pods. Select the beans that are smooth and firm, yet flexible. The tender beans are used in soups and salads, while the matured variety is used in rice and vegetable preparations. They are a good source of vitamin C and dietary fibre.

Okra (*bhindi*): Also known as ladies finger, this vegetable is firm and dark green with white edible seeds and ridged skin. Okra can be used to make salads as well as vegetable and yoghurt preparations. It is low in calories and fat, and is a great source of minerals, calcium and fibre.

Pointed gourd (*parwal*): This vegetable has green skin with white stripes, and pale white flesh with edible seeds. It can be used in soups, vegetable preparations and desserts. It is a rich source of copper, potassium, carbohydrates and vitamins A and C.

Ridged gourd (*turai*): This vegetable is dark green in colour with white flesh and edible seeds. It has a mild flavour and is rich in dietary fibre. It is a low-calorie vegetable and makes you feel full faster, thus helping in weight loss. It is a good source of vitamin C, zinc and iron.

Zucchini: This vegetable has shiny and edible outer skin. It is available in green and yellow varieties. Zucchini can be made into soup, salads and side dishes. Over-cooking can spoil the flavour and texture. It is a good source of potassium and B-complex vitamins.

ROOT VEGETABLES

Beetroot (*chukandar*): This vegetable is also known as table beet. It has cone-shape heads and is purple in colour. It is usually steamed, boiled or even eaten raw when combined with salad greens. It is a good source of fibre, vitamin C and magnesium. It is good for regulating blood sugar levels and helps to maintain muscle and bone strength.

Carrot (*gajar*): This long, cylindrical root vegetable can range in colour from orange to red to purple. Carrots after cooking not only retain their healthy properties but also their nutritive value. They are a good source of carotene, vitamins and minerals.

Colocasia (*arvi*): Also known as taro root, it is a round, elongated, heavy and tuberous root vegetable. After cooking, it imparts a nutty flavour. Colocasia can be steamed and made into dry and gravy vegetable preparations. This root contains good amounts of fibre and hence helps in the digestion process.

Ginger (*adrak*): This knobbly root is pale beige, with smooth skin and fibrous flesh. It has a warm, peppery flavour and robust aroma. It is an integral part of Indian cooking, especially when making pulses, pilafs, curries and masala tea. It is a versatile root and a good source of antioxidants.

Mango ginger (*aambahaldi*): This unique spice has smooth beige skin with off-white flesh inside. It looks like ginger but imparts a raw mango flavour. It is popularly used in India for making pickle, and has antioxidant and anti-fungal properties.

Potato (*aloo*): This starchy, tuberous vegetable comes in a variety of shapes, sizes and colours. It is considered to be the most versatile vegetable and is available throughout the year. It is rich in carbohydrates and so should be used moderately in your diet.

Sweet potatoes (*shakarkandi*): Sweet potato is a starchy root vegetable. Its skin colour ranges from white to pink to reddish brown. Sweet potatoes can be baked, steamed and made into salads, snacks and vegetable preparations. They are a good source of dietary fibre, as well as vitamins B6 and C.

Turmeric root (*haldi*): This root is pale brown on the outside with roughly textured, saffron-coloured flesh inside. This can be made into fresh pickle, while its dried powder is commonly used in most Indian preparations. It has wound-healing properties and is a powerful antioxidant.

MISCELLANEOUS VEGETABLES

Baby onion (*choti pyaz*): Also known as pearl or button onion. Its pearl-shaped bulbs have thin, paper-like, inedible skin and can range in colour from white to pink. They have a sweet, delicate flavour and a delicious crunch. They are rich in dietary fibre and vitamin C.

Bell pepper (*Shimla mirch*): This bell-shaped vegetable comes in a variety of sizes and colours including green, red and yellow. It is firm with glossy skin and has a watery crunch. It is a versatile vegetable and can be stuffed and grilled, as well as added to soups, salads and pilafs. It is a good source of vitamins A and C.

Button mushroom (*khumb*): Mushrooms are fleshy fungi that come in a variety of shapes and sizes. The most commonly used in Indian cooking are cultivated white mushrooms. When fresh, they have white caps and firm white flesh. They can be used in dips, toppings, soups, salads and curries. Button mushrooms are high in fibre, vitamins and minerals.

Cauliflower (*phool gobi*): This vegetable has green leaves enveloping tightly-packed white florets that are attached to stout stalks. It can be used in soups, side dishes and rice preparations. Cauliflower is low in fat and high in dietary fibre and vitamin C.

Cherry tomato (*chote tamatar*): This is the smaller and sweeter version of regular tomatoes and are usually round or oblong with shiny smooth skin. They vary in colour from red to orange to yellow. Cherry tomatoes are either used whole or halved in salads or garnishings.

Eggplant (*baingan*): Also known as aubergine. This vegetable comes in various sizes and colours, from white to green to dark purple. They have edible skin, seeds and sponge-like white flesh. They can be grilled and used to make side dishes and rice preparations. They are rich in dietary fibre and antioxidants.

Garlic (*lasan*): Each garlic bulb is made up of many individual pearly white cloves. Raw garlic has a strong odour and flavour, further released when cooked or chopped. Usually, when paired with ginger, cooked garlic turns sweeter and less pungent. Garlic aids in treating colds and boosting digestion. It is a good source of maganese and antioxidants.

Indian water chestnut (*singhara*): This seasonal fruit has a firm triangular shape. Colour varies from green to red. It has white flesh and a mildly sweet taste. Water chestnuts can be had raw, steamed or pan fried, and used in soups, salads, pilafs and vegetable preparations. They are a rich source of fibre, vitamins and minerals.

Lemon (*nimbu*): Lemons are round with firm, glossy rinds that range in colour from green to bright yellow. Lemon juice is used extensively to pep up salads, fruits, curries and pilafs, and to make lemonade, the famous refreshing drink. Lemon juice helps treat indigestion, constipation, dental problems and even fever. It is rich in antioxidants and vitamin C.

Lotus stem (*kamal kakadi*): Also known as lotus root, it is beige in colour and has crunchy white flesh inside with hollow cubicles. Lotus stem can be steamed or pan fried, and used in salads, soups, pilafs and curries. It is high in vitamin C, dietary fibre and minerals.

Onion (*pyaz*): This fleshy, round vegetable has a paper-like covering and comes in many varieties including red, white and yellow. The most commonly used onions are red and are full of flavour. They are chopped and used to make different Indian curries, soups, salads, lentils and rice pilafs. They are a good source of dietary fibre and vitamin C.

Pumpkin (*kaddu*): This vegetable has shiny green and pale yellow ribbed skin. Its flesh colour varies from deep yellow to orange. Pumpkins can be steamed or roasted and are commonly used in soups and curries. They are a rich source of antioxidants and vitamin K.

Sweet corn kernels (*meethe bhutte ke daane*): Also known as sugar corn, these have a high sugar content. These golden yellow kernels are soft and can be eaten directly off the cob after steaming or grilling. They can be enjoyed in soups, salads and curries. They are a good source of carbohydrates.

Tomato (*tamatar*): Tomatoes are juicy and pulpy with smooth, shiny skin that range in colour from red to green to yellow. They are versatile and can be used in soups, salads, drinks, curries and pilafs. They are a good source of vitamins A, C and K, protein and dietary fibre.

DRINKS, SOUPS & SALADS

ALMOND STRAWBERRY MILK
Badami Strawberry Peya

INGREDIENTS

½ cup / 65 gm Strawberries
1½ tsp Honey
1 cup / 200 ml Chilled almond milk (*badam doodh*) (see pg. 226)

METHOD

• Wash the strawberries and pat them dry with a kitchen towel. Hull and slice them.

• Place the sliced strawberries, honey and almond milk in the jar of a mixer. Pulse for 10–15 seconds to combine.

• **To serve**, transfer the milk from the blender to a glass and serve chilled. Garnish with a strawberry slice, if desired.

PER SERVING	225 ML
Calories	90
Fat (grams)	2
Carbohydrates (grams)	14
Protein (grams)	2

• Strawberries are a great source of the anti-ageing vitamin C.

• Almond milk, which is a good source of protein, makes this a power-packed drink.

TANGY MINT LEMONADE
Zaikedaar Shikanji

INGREDIENTS

¹/₈ tsp Lemon (*nimbu*) zest
1 Tbsp Lemon juice
¼ tsp Black salt (*kala namak*)
8 (4 + 4) Mint (*pudina*) leaves
2 tsp Honey
¾ cup / 150 ml Chilled water
4 Ice cubes
2 Lemon slices, deseeded
A sprig of mint, to garnish

METHOD

- Choose a firm lemon with unblemished skin. Using a fine grater or a microplane, zest the lemon. Set aside the lemon zest.

- Place the lemon juice, black salt, lemon zest, 4 mint leaves and honey, along with 150 ml of chilled water, in the jar of a mixer. Blend on the lowest speed until well mixed.

- **To serve**, place ice cubes, one lemon slice and the remaining 4 mint leaves in a glass and pour in the lemonade. Garnish with the remaining slice of lemon and a sprig of mint and serve.

PER SERVING	225 ML
Calories	48
Fat (grams)	0
Carbohydrates (grams)	12
Protein (grams)	0

- This drink aids in controlling body temperature, digestion and balancing electrolytes.
- 60 per cent of the body is made up of water. The water in our body helps to regulate body temperature, aids in digestion and helps to transport water-soluble vitamins in the body. Therefore it is important to remain adequately hydrated.

FLAVOURED BUTTERMILK
Chaas

INGREDIENTS

$^1/_3$ cup / 65 gm low-fat
Yoghurt (*dahi*)
1 cup / 200 ml Water
$^1/_3$ tsp Black salt (*kala namak*)
$^1/_8$ tsp Green chillies (*hari mirch*),
chopped
3 sprigs of coriander (*dhaniya*)
2 Spinach (*palak*) leaves
$^1/_8$ tsp roasted Cumin (*bhuna jeera*) powder (see pg. 222),
to garnish
1 Green chilli, to garnish
A sprig of coriander, to garnish

METHOD

- Place the yoghurt, water, black salt and chopped green chillies in a mixer. Blend on the lowest speed until smooth.

- Add the coriander and spinach leaves and blend for a few seconds more to shred the leaves.

- Pour the buttermilk into a tall glass and garnish with the roasted cumin seeds.

- Garnish with a green chilli and a sprig of coriander, if desired.

PER SERVING	275 ML
Calories	34
Fat (grams)	1.5
Carbohydrates (grams)	3
Protein (grams)	2

- Yoghurt is a combination of protein and simple sugars, which makes for an ideal snack.

- Choose black salt over table salt as it aids in digestion and reduces flatulence.

COASTAL COOLER
Solkadhi

INGREDIENTS

1 ½ cup / 105 gm fresh Coconut (*nariyal*), grated (see pg. 210)
⅓ tsp Garlic (*lasan*), chopped
⅓ tsp Green chillies (*hari mirch*), chopped
½ tsp Cumin (*jeera*) seeds
½ cup / 100 ml Warm water
1 cup / 200 ml (½ + ½) Water
8 petals of Kokum
¼ tsp Black salt (*kala namak*)
Salt, to taste
⅛ tsp roasted Cumin (*bhuna jeera*) powder (see pg. 222)
2 tsp fresh Coriander (*dhaniya*) leaves, chopped
A sprig of coriander, to garnish

PER SERVING	100 ML
Calories	223
Fat (grams)	13
Carbohydrates (grams)	25
Protein (grams)	1.5

METHOD

• Blend the grated coconut, chopped garlic, green chillies and cumin seeds in a mixer, along with ½ cup (100 ml) of warm water, until smooth.

• Strain the mixture through a fine muslin cloth and add ½ cup of water to the strained coconut milk. Set aside.

• Place the kokum petals in a pan with ½ cup (100 ml) of water. Bring the water to a boil over low heat. Mash the leaves with the back of a spoon and simmer for two minutes. Cool, strain and set aside.

• Add the kokum water to the strained coconut milk. Add black salt, salt, roasted cumin powder and chopped coriander leaves. Mix well. Garnish with a sprig of coriander and serve.

• Coconut, though actually a source of fat, can also act like an easy-to-digest carbohydrate.

• Kokum is an excellent source of vitamin C and has a cooling effect on the body.

MANGO ALMOND SMOOTHIE
Aamrasi Thandai

INGREDIENTS
½ tsp Sweet basil (*sabja*) seeds
1½ Tbsp Water
½ cup / 80 gm Mangoes (*aam*), chopped
¾ cup / 150 ml Chilled almond milk (*badam doodh*) (see pg. 226)
2 tsp Dried figs (*anjeer*), finely chopped
4–6 Ice cubes

METHOD
• Soak ½ tsp of sweet basil seeds in 1½ Tbsp of water for 5 minutes and set aside.

• Place the chopped mango, almond milk and chopped figs in a mixer. Blend at the lowest speed until smooth.

• **To serve**, place the ice cubes in a glass, add the soaked sweet basil seeds and pour in the blended mango almond milk. Some of the chopped fruit can be placed in the drink as a garnish.

PER SERVING	250 ML
Calories	110
Fat (grams)	2
Carbohydrates (grams)	21
Protein (grams)	2

• Mangoes are called the king of fruits for their numerous health benefits. They are a great source of beta carotene, also known as pro vitamin A, which helps boost immunity.

• Sabja seeds, also known as sweet basil seeds, add a nice crunch to the smoothie and balance the heating effect of the mangoes.

NUTTY BANANA COOLER
Badami Kela Thandai

INGREDIENTS
10 Almonds (*badam*)
I cup / 200 ml chilled,
low-fat Milk
1/3 cup / 40 gm ripe Banana
(*kela*) slices
1/8 tsp Cinnamon (*dalchini*)
powder

METHOD
- Grind the almonds at the lowest speed in a mixer to a thick paste. Remove and set aside.

- Blend the milk, banana slices, almond paste and cinnamon powder in a mixer. Blend on the lowest speed until smooth.

- Pour into a glass and serve immediately.

PER SERVING	250 ML
Calories	365
Fat (grams)	21
Carbohydrates (grams)	28
Protein (grams)	16

- Fully ripe bananas are a good source of the antioxidant known as glutathione.

- Almonds are a good source of protein and the antioxidant vitamin E.

PAPAYA-COCO SHAKE
Papita-Nariyal Sherbet

INGREDIENTS

3 Tbsp fresh Coconut (*nariyal*), grated (see pg. 210)
½ cup / 100 ml Water
1 cup / 145 gm Papaya (*papita*), peeled, deseeded and finely chopped
1 tsp Honey
A few papaya cubes, to garnish
A slice of lemon (*nimbu*), to garnish
A sprig of curry leaves (*kadhipatta*), to garnish

METHOD

• Grind the grated coconut with ½ cup of water at the lowest speed in a mixer until smooth. Strain and set aside the coconut milk.

• Place the chopped papaya, coconut milk and honey in a mixer. Blend until smooth.

• Transfer to a glass and serve garnished with a few papaya pieces, a lemon slice and a sprig of curry leaves.

PER SERVING	200 ML
Calories	198
Fat (grams)	10
Carbohydrates (grams)	25
Protein (grams)	2

• Papaya is a good source of the antioxidant vitamin A, which has many benefits, including maintaining healthy eye-sight.

PURE & SIMPLE ABC JUICE
Seeda Sada ABC Juice

INGREDIENTS

½ cup / 50 gm Apple (*seb*), peeled and chopped

6 Baby spinach (*palak*) leaves, roughly chopped

¼ cup (30 gm) Cucumber (*khira*), peeled and chopped

2 Tbsp fresh Coriander (*dhaniya*) leaves

1 tsp Lemon (*nimbu*) juice

¼ tsp Black salt (*kala namak*)

⅔ cup (135 ml) Water

A few apple slices, to garnish

A sprig of fresh coriander, to garnish

METHOD

- Place the chopped apple, spinach leaves, cucumber, coriander leaves, lemon juice, black salt and water in a mixer.

- Blend on the lowest speed to a slightly coarse texture.

- Transfer to a glass, garnish with apple slices and a sprig of coriander. Serve immediately.

PER SERVING	225 ML
Calories	72
Fat (grams)	0
Carbohydrates (grams)	17
Protein (grams)	0

- Packed with fruits, vegetables and greens, this juice is a great way to start your morning.

- It is important to blend at the lowest speed to avoid the mixer's motor from heating up and transferring heat to the juice, which may reduce its nutritional value.

SUMMER COOLER
Mast Mast Sherbet

Serves: 3 (675 ml)
Suggested portion per serving: 225 ml

PER SERVING	225 ML
Calories	24
Fat (grams)	0
Carbohydrates (grams)	5
Protein (grams)	1

INGREDIENTS

1½ tsp Ginger, chopped
3 Tbsp levelled / 30 gm Roasted black gram (*sattu*) powder
3 cups / 600 ml Water
Salt, to taste
¼ tsp Black salt (*kala namak*)
1½ tsp Ginger (*adrak*) juice
1 Tbsp Lemon (*nimbu*) juice
½ tsp *Chaat masala* (see pg. 222)
¼ tsp roasted Cumin (*bhuna jeera*) powder (see pg. 222)
3 Green chillies (*hari mirch*), slit and deseeded
1 Tbsp Coriander (*dhaniya*) leaves, finely chopped
4 Ice cubes, to serve
Sprig of coriander (*dhaniya*), to garnish

METHOD

• Place 1½ tsp chopped ginger and 1 Tbsp water in a mortar and pound to a coarse paste with a pestle. Collect the pulp with the help of the pestle on one side and use the residual ginger juice for the drink.

• Place the roasted black gram / *sattu* powder in a large pan. Add 1½ (300 ml) cups of water and whisk well. Now add the remaining 1½ (300 ml) cups of water and whisk again to combine.

• Add the salt, black salt, ginger juice, lemon juice, *chaat masala*, roasted cumin powder, deseeded green chillies and chopped coriander leaves. Whisk well and refrigerate.

• **To serve**, whisk the roasted black gram mixture well. Place 4 cubes of ice in a glass and pour in the chilled juice. Garnish with a sprig of fresh coriander.

• Roasted black gram powder (*sattu*) is an excellent source of protein.

• During summer months, *sattu* is a great digestive aid because of its cooling qualities.

TENDER COCONUT BREEZER
Harayali Daab Sherbet

INGREDIENTS

½ tsp Sweet basil (*sabja*) seeds
1½ Tbsp Water
1¼ cup / 250 ml Fresh coconut water (*daab*)
2 Tbsp Kiwi fruit, chopped
2 Tbsp English cucumber (*hara khira*), chopped

METHOD

• Soak the sweet basil seeds in 1½ Tbsp of water for 5 minutes and set aside.

• Pour the coconut water into a tall glass.

• Add the chopped kiwi fruit, soaked sweet basil seeds and chopped cucumber. Stir well and serve.

PER SERVING	275 ML
Calories	44
Fat (grams)	0
Carbohydrates (grams)	9
Protein (grams)	2

• Coconut water is good for hydration and an excellent source of potassium.

• Chia seeds can be used as a substitute to *subja* seeds.

WATERMELON PUNCH
Tarbooz Ka Sherbet

INGREDIENTS

1 cup / 150 gm Watermelon (*tarbooz*), deseeded, cut into small pieces
6 Mint (*pudina*) leaves
Pinch, Black salt (*kala namak*)
Thinly sliced watermelon wedge, to garnish
A sprig of mint, to garnish

METHOD

• Place the watermelon pieces, along with the mint leaves and black salt, in a mixer.

• Blend until smooth on the lowest setting.

• Transfer to a glass and serve garnished with a thin watermelon wedge and a sprig of mint.

PER SERVING	150 ML
Calories	167
Fat (grams)	0
Carbohydrates (grams)	31
Protein (grams)	3

• Watermelon, if consumed on an empty stomach, may cause indigestion. Adding black salt is an easy way to combat this and other digestive issues.

EVERGREEN SOUP
Hara Bhara Shorba

INGREDIENTS

1 tsp Rice bran oil
½ tsp Ginger (*adrak*), finely chopped
½ tsp Garlic (*lasan*), finely chopped
⅔ cup / 60 gm Broccoli florets, cut into ½-inch pieces
1 cup / 110 gm Zucchini, cut into 1-inch slant pieces (see pg. 215)
4 Tbsp Bean sprouts (*ankurit moong*) (see pg. 217)
2 tsp Celery, finely chopped (see pg. 216)
Salt, to taste
2 cup / 400 ml Water
⅛ tsp freshly ground Black peppercorn (*sabut kali mirch*)
15 Baby spinach leaves (*chote palak ke patte*)
¼ tsp Lemon (*nimbu*) juice

METHOD

- Heat 1 tsp oil in a broad pan for 30 seconds over medium heat. Add the chopped ginger and garlic and sauté for 10 seconds. Add broccoli, zucchini, bean sprouts, celery and a pinch of salt. Mix and sauté for 30 seconds.

- Add 2 cups / 400 ml of water, black pepper powder and salt. Bring the mixture to a boil, add the spinach leaves and mix well. Turn off the heat and add the lemon juice. Mix and serve immediately.

PER SERVING	300 ML
Calories	58
Fat (grams)	2
Carbohydrates (grams)	6
Protein (grams)	4

- Vegetables are not only a great source of vitamins and minerals – they also contain large amounts of fibre which, along with fluids, help maintain a healthy digestive system.

BABY BOK CHOY & ONION SOUP
Pattidar Shorba

INGREDIENTS

4 heads of Baby bok choy
4 Spring onion (*hara pyaz*) bulbs
1 tsp Rice bran oil
1 tsp Ginger (*adrak*) paste (see pg. 212)
1 tsp Garlic (*lasan*) paste (see pg. 212)
2 tsp Coriander stems, finely chopped (*kache danthal*) (see pg. 216)
2½ cups / 500 ml Water
Salt, to taste
Freshly ground Black peppercorn (*sabut kali mirch*), to taste
Lemon (*nimbu*) juice

METHOD

- Separate the leaves and the stem of the bok choy. Keep leaves aside. Cut the stem into 1½-inch slant pieces. This should make ½ cup of chopped bok choy.

- Peel the onion bulbs and cut into thin, round slices. This should make ¼ cup of sliced onions.

- Heat 1 tsp oil in a broad pan for 30 seconds over medium heat. Add the ginger paste, garlic paste, chopped coriander stem, chopped bok choy stems and onion slices. Sauté for 10 seconds.

- Add the bok choy leaves (2 cups) and cook for 30 seconds. Now add 2½ cups / 500 ml water, salt and black pepper. Bring this mixture to a boil. Add the chopped coriander leaves and lemon juice, and serve hot.

PER SERVING	300 ML
Calories	54
Fat (grams)	3
Carbohydrates (grams)	3
Protein (grams)	2

- Bok choy is an excellent source of folic acid, which is vital for pregnant women as it helps prevent neural tube defects in newborn babies.

BLACK CHICKPEA SOUP
Kaale Chane Ka Shorba

INGREDIENTS

¼ cup / 45 gm Black chickpeas (*kala chana*)
3 cups / 600 ml Water
⅛ tsp Salt
1 tsp Rice bran oil
1 tsp Ginger (*adrak*) paste
(see pg. 212)
8 medium / 100 gm Button
mushroom (*khumb*), thinly sliced
Salt, to taste
⅛ tsp freshly ground Black
peppercorn (*sabut kali mirch*)
1 tsp Lemon (*nimbu*) juice
3 Tbsp Spring onion leaves (*hara pyaz ke patte*), finely chopped
(see pg. 216)

METHOD

• Wash and soak the black chickpeas in water overnight or for 10 hours. Drain and set aside.

• In a pressure cooker, add the black chickpeas, water and salt. Cook until one whistle. Reduce and simmer for 30 minutes. Turn off the heat and once the pressure settles, remove the lid and allow to cool for 5–10 minutes. Drain and reserve the stock to use in the soup.

• Heat 1 tsp oil in a broad pan for 30 seconds over medium heat. Add ginger paste and sliced mushroom and cook for 30 seconds. Add the chickpeas stock, salt and ground black pepper to taste. Add the lemon juice and mix well.

• **To serve**, in a soup bowl, add 3 Tbsp of cooked black chickpeas and 1½ Tbsp of chopped spring onion leaves. Pour the hot soup over it. Serve immediately.

PER SERVING	250 ML
Calories	103
Fat (grams)	3
Carbohydrates (grams)	13
Protein (grams)	6

• Nutrients get leached by water when ingredients come in contact with it. Therefore it is beneficial to use the liquid/stock in which ingredients are cooked.

BUTTON MUSHROOM SOUP
Khumb Shorba

INGREDIENTS

200 gm (100 + 100) Button mushrooms (*khumb*)
2 tsp (1 + 1) Rice bran oil
1 / 60 gm Onion (*pyaz*), finely chopped
1½ cups / 250 ml (1 + ½) Water
2 tsp Garlic (*lasan*), chopped
1 cup / 200 ml low-fat Milk
¹/₈ tsp freshly ground Black peppercorn (*sabut kali mirch*)
Salt, to taste
1 Tbsp chopped Celery (see pg. 216)
A sprig of celery leaf, to garnish

METHOD

- Cut 100 grams of mushroom into small pieces and set aside.

- Cut the remaining 100 grams of mushroom into thin slices and set aside.

- Heat 1 tsp of oil in a broad pan for 30 seconds over medium heat. Add the chopped onion and sauté for 30 seconds. Add the 100 grams of chopped mushrooms and sauté for another 30 seconds until they shrink a little. Add 1 cup / 200 ml of water. Give it a good stir and turn off the heat.

- Once cool, blend in a mixer until completely smooth. Add the remaining ½ cup (50 ml) of water. Set aside this mushroom stock.

- Heat 1 tsp of oil in a broad pan for 30 seconds over medium heat. Add the chopped garlic and sauté for 10 seconds. Add the sliced mushrooms and cook for another 30 seconds.

- Add the mushroom stock, 1 cup (200 ml) of milk, ground black pepper, salt and chopped celery. Bring the soup to a boil and simmer for 2 minutes. Serve hot, garnished with a sprig of celery leaf.

PER SERVING	250 ML
Calories	145.5
Fat (grams)	5.5
Carbohydrates (grams)	16
Protein (grams)	8

- Mushrooms are one of the few vegetables that contain B vitamins, which help pull energy out of foods and enable the body to utilize it.

GARDEN SOUP
Sabz Shorba

INGREDIENTS

For the stock:
2 tsp (½ + 1½) Rice bran oil
2 Bay leaves (*tej patta*)
1 cup / 150 gm Potato (*aloo*),
cut into medium cubes
⅓ cup / 50 gm Carrot (*gajar*),
peeled, cut into ¼-inch discs
2½ cups / 500 ml Water
2 tsp Garlic (*lasan*), chopped
Salt, to taste
Freshly ground Black
peppercorn (*sabut kali mirch*),
to taste
1 tsp Lemon (*nimbu*) juice

Other ingredients:
½ cup / 75 gm Carrot (*gajar*),
finely chopped (see pg. 214),
steamed for a minute
4 Tbsp Bean sprouts (*ankurit
moong*) (see pg. 217)
2 tsp Celery, chopped
2 tsp Coriander (*dhaniya*) leaves,
finely chopped
2 Green chillies (*hari mirch*)
8 Sweet basil leaves

METHOD

• Heat ½ tsp of oil in a pressure cooker for 30 seconds over medium heat. Add the bay leaves, potato and carrot cubes. Mix well. Add water and pressure cook to one whistle. Turn off the heat and allow the pressure to settle.

• Open the lid, remove the bay leaves and let the mixture cool. Blend the mixture in a mixer until smooth. Set this stock aside.

• Heat 1½ tsp of oil in a broad pan for 30 seconds over medium heat. Add the chopped garlic and sauté for 10 seconds. Add the stock, salt and freshly ground black pepper. Mix and bring the soup to a boil. Add lemon juice and turn off the heat.

• **To serve,** divide the steamed carrots, bean sprouts, celery, coriander, green chillies and basil leaves between two soup bowls. Top each bowl with hot soup and serve immediately.

PER SERVING	300 ML
Calories	120
Fat (grams)	4
Carbohydrates (grams)	19
Protein (grams)	2

• It is advisable to blend the stock in batches to avoid spillage.

• Soups are a good addition to any weight management meal plan as they provide large quantities of nutritional value at a low calorie intake.

SPICED PUMPKIN SOUP
Kaddu Ka Shorba

INGREDIENTS

1 tsp (½ + ½) Rice bran oil
1 Star anise (*chakra phool*)
2 cups / 300 gm Pumpkin (*kaddu*), peeled and cut into 1-inch pieces
1½ cups / 300 ml Water
6 Haricot beans, finely chopped
⅛ tsp freshly ground Black peppercorn (*sabut kali mirch*), to taste
Salt, to taste
1 tsp Lemon (*nimbu*) juice
1 tsp Sunflower seeds (*surajmukhi ke beej*), to garnish

METHOD

- Heat ½ tsp of oil in a pressure cooker for 30 seconds over medium heat. Add the star anise, chopped pumpkin and water. Pressure cook to one whistle and turn off the heat. Once the pressure settles, remove the lid and cool.

- Once cool, remove the star anise and blend the cooked pumpkin mixture in a mixer until smooth. Strain this stock and set aside.

- Heat ½ tsp of oil in a broad pan for 30 seconds. Add the chopped haricot beans and sauté for 30 seconds. Now add the strained pumpkin stock, freshly ground pepper and salt. Mix well.

- Bring the soup to a boil and turn off the heat. Add lemon juice and mix well. Garnish with sunflower seeds and serve hot.

PER SERVING	250 ML
Calories	73
Fat (grams)	3
Carbohydrates (grams)	10
Protein (grams)	1.5

- Pumpkin is a healing food as it contains vitamin K, which is used by the body to help blood clotting.

SPLIT GREEN GRAM SOUP
Moong Daal Shorba

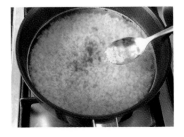

INGREDIENTS

2 Tbsp / 30 gm Skinned, split green gram (*dhuli moong daal*)
2½ cups / 500 ml Water
⅛ tsp Turmeric (*haldi*) powder
12 / 40 gm Haricot beans, cut into thin, slant pieces (see pg. 214)
½ cup / 75 gm Carrot (*gajar*), peeled and cut into small pieces (see pg. 214)
2 tsp Rice bran oil
½-inch Cinnamon (*dalchini*) stick
1 / 60 gm Onion (*pyaz*), cut into medium cubes (see pg. 215)
1 tsp Ginger (*adrak*), chopped
Salt, to taste
⅛ tsp freshly ground Black peppercorn (*sabut kali mirch*)
Pinch, Cinnamon (*dalchini*) powder
1 tsp Lemon (*nimbu*) juice

METHOD

- Wash and soak the split green gram lentil in water for 30 minutes. Drain and set aside.

- In a pan, bring the water to a boil. Add the soaked green gram lentil and turmeric powder. Bring to a boil. Simmer for 12 minutes or until the lentils are cooked *al dente* (with a slight bite to it). Set aside.

- Steam the beans and carrots in a vegetable steamer / double boiler for a minute (see pgs. 218–19). Remove and set aside.

- Heat 2 tsp oil in a broad pan for 30 seconds over medium heat. Add the cinnamon stick, onion cubes and chopped ginger and sauté until the onions become translucent. Add the steamed vegetables, mix and cook for 10 seconds. Now add the cooked green gram lentil, salt and black pepper powder. Bring to a boil and add the cinnamon powder and mix. Turn off the heat. Add lemon juice, mix well and serve immediately.

PER SERVING	250 ML
Calories	128
Fat (grams)	4
Carbohydrates (grams)	17
Protein (grams)	6

- Skinned, split green gram lentils help keep the stomach filled because of the protein content which takes longer to digest.

ROASTED BELL PEPPER SOUP
Bhuni Shimla Mirch Ka Shorba

INGREDIENTS

2 tsp (¼ + ¼ + 1½) Rice bran oil
2 / 250 gm Red bell peppers
(lal Shimla mirch)
4 / 110 gm Baby onions
(choti pyaz)
15 Sweet basil leaves
2 cups / 400 ml (1 + 1) Water
1 tsp Garlic (lasan), chopped
¾ cup / 15 gm loosely packed
Spinach (palak), chopped (see
pg. 216)
Salt, to taste
⅛ tsp freshly ground Black
peppercorn (sabut kali mirch)

METHOD

• Brush ¼ + ¼ tsp of oil on both the bell peppers. Roast each bell pepper over a stove flame until charred evenly. Immediately wrap in a kitchen towel and cover with a bowl. Set aside for 20 minutes. Unwrap and peel the bell peppers. Deseed and roughly chop them.

• Pierce each onion all over with a fork and roast over a stove flame until charred on the surface. Peel the charred layer, wipe with a kitchen towel and chop roughly.

• Coarsely blend the chopped bell peppers and onions along with the basil leaves and 1 cup (200 ml) of water in a mixer. Transfer to a bowl, add 1 (200 ml) cup of water and mix well. The stock is ready.

• Heat 1½ tsp of oil in a broad pan for 30 seconds. Add the chopped garlic and sauté for 10 seconds. Add the chopped spinach, stock, salt and freshly ground black pepper. Mix well and bring to a boil. Turn off the heat and serve hot.

PER SERVING	200 ML
Calories	42
Fat (grams)	2
Carbohydrates (grams)	6
Protein (grams)	0

• Covering the roasted bell pepper immediately in a kitchen towel after roasting will help moisten the skin enough to peel off easily.

• Red bell peppers are a superfood as they contain large amounts of the antioxidant vitamin C.

BROCCOLI SOUP
Hari Phoolgobi Ka Shorba

Serves: 2 (500 ml)
Suggested portion per serving: 250 ml

INGREDIENTS

2 cups / 180 gm Broccoli florets, cut into ½-inch pieces
2 cups / 400 (1 + 1) low-fat Milk
2 tsp Rice bran oil
¼ tsp Garlic (*lasan*), chopped
2 Tbsp Sweet corn kernels (*meethe bhutte ke daane*)
Salt, to taste
$1/8$ tsp freshly ground Black peppercorn (*sabut kali mirch*)
¼ tsp ($1/8 + 1/8$) Flax seeds (*alsi ke beej*), to garnish
2 Parsley leaves (1 + 1), to garnish

METHOD

- Steam the broccoli florets in a double boiler / vegetable steamer for 3 minutes (see pgs. 218–19). Remove and set aside to cool.

- Blend the florets with 1 cup / 200 ml of milk in a mixer. Blend on the lowest speed until smooth.

- Heat 2 tsp oil in a broad pan for 30 seconds over medium heat. Add the chopped garlic and sauté for 10 seconds. Add the sweet corn kernels and sauté for another 20 seconds.

- Now add the remaining 1 cup / 200 ml of milk, salt and pepper, and the blended broccoli mixture. Bring the soup to a boil and simmer for 30 seconds.

- Serve hot, garnished with flax seeds and parsley leaves.

PER SERVING	250 ML
Calories	207
Fat (grams)	7
Carbohydrates (grams)	24
Protein (grams)	12

- Broccoli is a good source of calcium. This recipe, where broccoli is paired with milk, provides almost an entire day's recommended amount of calcium.

WATERMELON SALAD
Tarbooz Ka Salaad

INGREDIENTS

2 cups / 300 gm Watermelon
(*tarbooz*), deseeded, cut into
1-inch cubes
3 cups / 105 gm Iceberg lettuce,
torn into 2-inch pieces
2 tsp Black olive, sliced
25 gm Feta cheese, cut into
½-inch cubes (see pg. 180)
20 Sweet basil leaves
1 Tbsp Pine nuts (*chilgoza*)

For the dressing:

1 Tbsp Balsamic vinegar
1 tsp Extra virgin olive oil
1 tsp Honey
¼ tsp Red chilli (*lal mirch*) flakes
¼ tsp freshly ground Black
peppercorn (*sabut kali mirch*)
1 tsp Whole grain mustard
sauce (*kasundi* sauce)
¼ tsp Salt

METHOD

- Cover the cut watermelon pieces with cling film and refrigerate until chilled. Next, cover the lettuce with cling film and refrigerate until chilled.

- Rinse the olive slices in water, drain and set aside.

- Make the dressing by whisking together all the listed ingredients in a bowl. Whisk well and set aside.

- Next, assemble the salad. Place the lettuce leaves on a mixing plate and arrange the watermelon pieces over the leaves. Give the dressing a good stir and drizzle it over the salad. Top it with feta cheese, olive slices and basil leaves. Toss gently.

- Garnish with pine nuts. Serve chilled.

PER SERVING	1¾ CUP
Calories	124
Fat (grams)	8
Carbohydrates (grams)	10
Protein (grams)	3

- *Kasundi* is a speciality mustard sauce from the Bengal region of India.
- Feta cheese, along with sweet basil leaves, gives this salad a good dose of calcium.

BEETROOT SALAD
Chukandar Ka Salaad

INGREDIENTS

2 / 150 gm Beetroot
(*chukandar*)
1½ cups / 300 ml Water
2 cups / 45 gm tightly packed
Baby spinach leaves (*chote palak
ke patte*)
½ cup / 12 gm Sweet basil leaves
1 cup / 80 gm Fenugreek
(*methi*) sprouts (see pg. 217)
2 Tbsp Sunflower seeds
(*surajmukhi ke beej*)

For the dressing:
1¼ Tbsp Balsamic vinegar
2 tsp whole grain Mustard sauce
(*kasundi* sauce)
1 tsp Honey
¼ tsp Red chilli (*lal mirch*)
powder
¼ tsp Salt

METHOD

- Wash the beetroots well and place them on a cooking rack in a pressure cooker. Add 1½ cups / 300 ml water. Pressure cook over high heat to one whistle and then simmer for 7 minutes. Turn off the heat and allow the pressure to settle. Remove the beetroot from the pressure cooker. Once cool, peel and cut them into ⅛-inch semi-circular slices.

- Cover the sliced beetroot, spinach, basil leaves and fenugreek sprouts with cling film and refrigerate until chilled.

- Make the dressing by whisking together all the listed ingredients in a bowl. Whisk well and set aside.

- **To serve**, arrange half the baby spinach leaves, beetroot slices, basil leaves, fenugreek sprouts and sunflower seeds on a serving plate. Give the dressing a good mix and drizzle half of it over the arranged salad.

- Top with the remaining beetroot slices, spinach, basil leaves and fenugreek sprouts. Drizzle the remaining dressing evenly over the salad and garnish with the remaining sunflower seeds. Serve immediately.

PER SERVING	1½ CUP
Calories	79
Fat (grams)	3
Carbohydrates (grams)	8
Protein (grams)	5

- Cooked beetroot contains a higher amount of simple sugars, making it an excellent source of immediate energy.

- Sunflower seeds help control blood sugar levels, making this recipe
  ideal for weight management.

BLACK RICE & AVOCADO SALAD
Chawal Ki Tirangi Salaad

INGREDIENTS

1 cup / 150 gm Tomato
(*tamatar*), cut into medium
cubes, deseeded
1 cup / 125 gm Yellow bell
pepper (*pili Shimla mirch*), cut
into medium cubes
1 cup / 50 gm Spring onion
leaves (*hara pyaz ke patte*),
finely chopped
½ cup / 90 gm Black rice
(*kaale chawal*)

For the dressing:
1 medium / 250 gm ripe
Avocado (*makhan fal*)
3 tsp Garlic (*lasan*), chopped
1 tsp Extra virgin olive oil
¼ tsp Red chilli (*lal mirch*) flakes
4 tsp Lemon (*nimbu*) juice
¾ tsp Salt

METHOD

• Cover the cut tomato, yellow bell pepper and spring onion with cling film and refrigerate until chilled.

• Wash the rice and soak it in water for 1 hour. Drain in a colander.

• Boil 1 cup / 200 ml water in a broad pan. Add the drained rice and bring to a boil. Cover the pan and simmer for 20–30 minutes, or until the rice is cooked through (see pg. 220). Set the rice aside.

• Cut the avocado in half lengthwise and remove the pit (see pg. 210). With a spoon, gently scoop out the avocado flesh and set aside.

• In a mortar and pestle, pound the chopped garlic well. Add the avocado flesh a few teaspoons at a time and pound to make a smooth paste. Transfer to a bowl.

• Add olive oil, red chilli flakes, lemon juice and salt to the avocado to make a dressing. Mix well.

• **To serve,** mix the cooked black rice with the avocado dressing. Add the chilled vegetables and mix well. Serve immediately.

PER SERVING	¾ CUP
Calories	173
Fat (grams)	9
Carbohydrates (grams)	17
Protein (grams)	9

• Black rice contains iron, which, when combined with a source of vitamin C such as yellow bell peppers, helps increase the absorption of iron by the body.

• Avocados are a great source of heart-healthy monounsaturated fats.

GARDEN SALAD
Hari Bhari Salaad

INGREDIENTS

1¼ cups / 93 gm Broccoli
florets, cut into 1-inch pieces
½ cup / 60 gm Yellow bell
pepper (*pili Shimla mirch*) cubes,
¾-inch pieces
1½ cup / 15 gm tightly packed,
mixed Romaine lettuce
10 Almonds (*badam*), slivered
and roasted (see pg. 208),
to garnish

For the dressing:

2 tsp Balsamic vinegar
1 tsp whole grain Mustard sauce
(*kasundi* sauce)
½ tsp Jaggery (*gur*) powder
¼ tsp Salt
1/8 tsp Red chilli (*lal mirch*)
powder

METHOD

- Steam the broccoli florets in
  a double boiler / vegetable
  steamer for 2 minutes (see
  pgs. 218–19). Remove and set
  aside to cool.

- Roughly tear the salad leaves
  to 2-inch pieces and set aside.

- Cover the broccoli, yellow
  bell pepper and lettuce with
  cling film and refrigerate
  until chilled.

- Make the dressing by whisking
  together all the listed
  ingredients in a bowl.
  Whisk well and set aside.

- **To serve**, place half the
  lettuce leaves, bell peppers
  and broccoli florets in a
  serving plate. Give the
  dressing a good stir and
  drizzle half onto the salad.
  Add the remaining salad
  leaves, bell peppers and
  broccoli florets and drizzle
  the remaining dressing over it.
  Toss gently and serve.

- Garnish with the roasted
  almonds and serve.

PER SERVING	2¼ CUP
Calories	87
Fat (grams)	3
Carbohydrates (grams)	10
Protein (grams)	5

- Beginning a meal with a fibre-packed salad helps to keep the
  stomach full for longer without consuming large amounts of calories.

MIXED GREEN GRAM SALAD
Kosambari

INGREDIENTS

1 cup / 120 gm English cucumber (*hara khira*), cut into medium size cubes

¼ cup / 45 gm Skinned, split green gram (*dhuli moong dal*)

1 cup / 150 gm Tomato (*tamatar*), deseeded, cut into medium size cubes (see pg. 224)

2 tsp Ginger (*adrak*), finely chopped

¼ tsp Green chillies (*hari mirch*), finely chopped

3 tsp Lemon (*nimbu*) juice

2 Tbsp fresh Coriander (*dhaniya*) leaves, finely chopped

Salt, to taste

2 Tbsp fresh Coconut (*nariyal*), grated (see pg. 210), to garnish

For the tempering:

2 tsp Rice bran oil

¼ tsp Mustard (*sarson*) seeds

10 Curry leaves (*kadhipatta*)

METHOD

• Wash and soak the split green gram in water for 3 hours.

• Drain and spread on a kitchen towel to dry. Set aside.

• Mix the skinned, split green gram lentil with chopped cucumber, tomatoes, ginger, green chillies, lemon juice, coriander leaves and salt. Transfer to a serving bowl.

• Heat the oil in a tempering ladle for 30 seconds. Add the mustard seeds and, when they splutter, add the curry leaves. Pour immediately over the salad.

• Garnish with grated coconut and serve.

PER SERVING	1¼ CUP
Calories	156
Fat (grams)	7.2
Carbohydrates (grams)	16
Protein (grams)	4.5

• Uncooked lentils have three times the amount of protein found in cooked lentils.

• If substituting English cucumber with Indian cucumber, peel and deseed to allow for easier digestion.

LOTUS STEM & ZUCCHINI SALAD
Kamal Kakdi Aur Zucchini Salaad

INGREDIENTS

1 / 150 gm Lotus stem (*kamal kakdi*), peeled and cut into 1-inch diagonal pieces (see pg. 214)
1½ cups / 300 ml Water
1¼ tsp (½ + ½ + ¼) Rice bran oil
1 / 140 gm Zucchini, cut into 1-inch diagonal pieces (see pg. 215)
50 gm Cherry tomatoes (*chote tamatar*), halved
2 cups / 70 gm Iceberg lettuce, torn into 2-inch pieces, refrigerated until chilled
Handful of parsley, to garnish

For the dressing:

1½ Tbsp Balsamic vinegar
1 tsp whole grain Mustard sauce (*kasundi* sauce)
1 tsp Honey
⅓ tsp Salt
⅛ tsp freshly ground Black peppercorn (*sabut kali mirch*)
⅛ tsp Red chilli (*lal mirch*) flakes

METHOD

• Place the cut lotus stem pieces in a small colander that fits into a pressure cooker. Set aside.

• Add 1½ cups / 300 ml of water to a pressure cooker. Place the colander with the lotus stem on a cooking rack inside the pressure cooker. Pressure cook over high heat until one whistle. Turn off the heat and let the pressure settle (see pg. 213). Remove the colander and allow the lotus stem to cool.

• Heat a griddle (*tawa*) over medium heat for 30 seconds and brush it with ¼ tsp of oil. Arrange the lotus stem pieces on the griddle and brush the pieces with ¼ tsp oil. Grill for 2 minutes on both sides over medium heat. Remove and set aside.

• Brush the griddle with ¼ tsp of oil and arrange the zucchini pieces on it. Brush the zucchini with ¼ tsp of oil and grill for a minute on both sides. Remove and set aside.

• Brush the griddle with ¼ tsp of oil and arrange the cherry tomatoes (cut side facing down). Grill for a minute. Remove and set aside.

• Make the dressing by whisking together all the listed ingredients in a bowl. Whisk well and set aside.

• **To serve,** place half the lettuce leaves, lotus stem, zucchini pieces and half of the cherry tomatoes in a mixing plate. Give the dressing a good stir and drizzle half of it over the salad. Add the remaining salad leaves, lotus stem, zucchini and cherry tomatoes. Drizzle the remaining dressing over it. Toss gently, garnish with parsley and serve.

PER SERVING	1 CUP HEAP
Calories	61
Fat (grams)	1
Carbohydrates (grams)	12
Protein (grams)	1

• Retain the crisp freshness in lettuce leaves by dunking them into a big bowl of ice cold water for several minutes.

• Lotus stems are often muddy inside, therefore select ones with closed ends.

NUTTY SPINACH SALAD
Thandi Palak Salaad

INGREDIENTS

250 gm Baby spinach (*chote palak ke patte*)

1 cup / 100 gm Red bell pepper (*lal shimla mirch*), finely sliced to 1-inch pieces

1 tsp Sesame (*til*) seeds, roasted (see pg. 211), to garnish

For the dressing:

2 Tbsp Peanuts (*moongphalli*)

¼ tsp Red chilli (*lal mirch*) powder

¼ tsp Salt

½ tsp Jaggery (*gur*)

2 tsp White vinegar

¼ tsp Rice (*chawal*) flour

½ cup / 100 ml (¼ + ¼) Water

METHOD

- Trim the edges of the spinach, wash and drain in a colander. Stack the baby spinach in a double boiler / vegetable steamer and steam for a minute. Remove and gently pat dry with a kitchen towel.

- Transfer to a dish, cover with cling film and refrigerate until chilled.

- **For the dressing**, pre-heat the oven at 180°C. In a baking tray, roast the peanuts for 3–4 minutes or until light golden brown. Remove and set aside to cool.

- In a mixer, grind the roasted peanuts with red chilli powder, salt, jaggery, white vinegar and ¼ cup / 50 ml of water into a fine paste.

- In a pan, mix ¼ cup / 50 ml of water with ¼ tsp rice flour. Add the peanut paste and bring the mixture to a boil over medium heat, stirring continuously. Set aside to cool.

- Make the dressing by whisking together all the listed ingredients in a bowl. Whisk well and set aside.

- **To serve,** divide the spinach and red bell pepper into two portions. Stack half the spinach on a serving plate and arrange half of the red bell pepper slices on top. Spoon half of the dressing over it. Now arrange the remaining spinach and cut the salad into six equal portions with a sharp knife (cutting spinach into 6 equal portions makes it easy to serve). Top with the remaining bell pepper slices and dressing. Garnish with the roasted sesame seeds and serve chilled.

PER SERVING	1 CUP
Calories	72
Fat (grams)	1.8
Carbohydrates (grams)	7.3
Protein (grams)	3.3

- The vitamin C from the red bell peppers will help increase the absorption of iron from the spinach.

- Try using black jaggery, which is also a good source of iron.

POMELO SALAD
Chakotara Ka Salaad

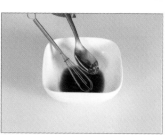

INGREDIENTS

1½ cup / 210 gm Pomelo segments (*chakotara*), cut into 1-inch pieces (see pg. 210)
¾ cup / 90 gm Yellow bell pepper (*pili Shimla mirch*), cut into 1-inch squares
½ cup / 25 gm Spring onion leaves (*hara pyaz ke patte*), finely chopped (see pg. 216)
2 Tbsp fresh Coriander (*dhaniya*) leaves, finely chopped
20 Sweet basil leaves
½ tsp Sesame (*til*) seeds, roasted (see pg. 211), to garnish

For the dressing:
2 tsp Sesame oil
2 tsp Honey
⅛ tsp Red chilli (*lal mirch*) flakes
⅓ tsp Black salt (*kala namak*)
⅛ tsp freshly ground Black peppercorn (*sabut kali mirch*)

METHOD

- Cover the cut pomelo segments, yellow bell pepper and spring onion with cling film and refrigerate until chilled.

- To serve, place the pomelo, yellow bell pepper, spring onion and basil in a mixing bowl.

- Make the dressing by whisking together all the listed ingredients in a bowl. Whisk well and drizzle over the salad.

- Toss gently and transfer to a serving dish. Garnish with the roasted sesame seeds and serve immediately.

PER SERVING	1 CUP
Calories	90
Fat (grams)	2
Carbohydrates (grams)	15
Protein (grams)	3

- The combination of pomelo and yellow bell peppers makes for a great immunity-boosting salad packed with vitamin C.

- Sesame oil contains almost the same amount of both heart-healthy monounsaturated and polyunsaturated fat.

SPROUTED MOTH BEAN SALAD
Moth Ki Ankurit Salaad

INGREDIENTS

2½ cups / 250 gm Moth bean sprouts (*ankurit moth*)

1 cup / 50 gm Spring onion leaves (*hara pyaz ke patte*), finely chopped (see pg. 216)

1 cup / 150 gm Carrots (*gajar*), finely chopped

2 tsp Ginger (*adrak*), finely chopped

2 Tbsp fresh Coriander (*dhaniya*) leaves, finely chopped

¼ cup / 37.2 gm Peanuts (*moongphalli*), roasted, skinned (see pg. 211), to garnish

1–2 sprigs of coriander, to garnish

For the dressing:

4 tsp Lemon (*nimbu*) juice

½ tsp Salt

½ tsp *Chaat masala* (see pg. 222)

⅛ tsp Red chilli (*lal mirch*) powder

METHOD

- Steam the moth bean sprouts in a double boiler / vegetable steamer for 2 minutes (see pgs. 218–19). Remove and set aside to cool.

- Make the dressing by whisking together all the listed ingredients in a bowl. Whisk well and set aside.

- **To serve**, mix the moth bean sprouts, chopped spring onion leaves, carrots, ginger and chopped coriander leaves. Pour the dressing and toss gently.

- Garnish with the roasted peanuts and sprigs of coriander, and serve.

PER SERVING	1 CUP
Calories	194
Fat (grams)	6
Carbohydrates (grams)	25
Protein (grams)	10

- Sprouting beans and whole lentils significantly increases the iron content.

- Vitamin C from the lemon juice helps increase the absorption of iron.

ROASTED PUMPKIN SALAD
Bhuna Kaddu Ka Mila-Jula Salaad

INGREDIENTS

¾ cup / 75 gm Red apple (*lal seb*) thinly sliced to 1-inch pieces
1 tsp Lemon (*nimbu*) juice
1 tsp Rice bran oil
1 cup / 135 gm Yellow pumpkin (*kaddu*), cut into 1-inch pieces with ½-inch width
Pinch, salt
3 cups / 105 gm Iceberg lettuce, torn into 2-inch pieces
¾ cup / 90 gm Cucumber (*khira*) peeled, cut into ¾-inch pieces
1½ Tbsp Pumpkin seeds (*kaddu ke beej*), to garnish

For the dressing:
3 tsp Sesame (*til*) seeds
2 Tbsp Yoghurt (*dahi*), whisked
1½ tsp Honey
1½ tsp White vinegar
¼ tsp Black salt (*kala namak*)
¼ tsp freshly ground Black peppercorn (*sabut kali mirch*)

METHOD

- Toss the apple slices with 1 tsp lemon juice, cover with cling film and refrigerate until chilled.

- In a bowl, cover the lettuce and cucumber pieces with cling film and refrigerate until chilled.

- Heat a griddle (*tawa*) and brush it with ½ tsp of oil. Arrange the pumpkin pieces on the griddle and brush them with the remaining ½ tsp of oil. Sprinkle a pinch a salt, cover with a lid and cook over low heat for 10 minutes on each side. Remove and set aside.

- To make the dressing, heat a pan over medium heat for 10 seconds. Add sesame seeds. Stir frequently until the seeds are light golden brown. Set aside to cool.

- In a mixer, pulse the sesame seeds to a powder. Do not grind for too long, as the seeds will begin to release their oil.

- Whisk together the roasted sesame powder, yoghurt, honey, white vinegar, black salt and freshly ground black pepper. Refrigerate.

- **To serve**, place the lettuce on a mixing plate and add the pumpkin, apple and cucumber pieces. Give the dressing a good stir and drizzle over the salad. Toss gently and transfer to a serving dish.

- Garnish with pumpkin seeds and serve immediately.

PER SERVING	1¾ CUP
Calories	117
Fat (grams)	3
Carbohydrates (grams)	18.5
Protein (grams)	4

- Cucumbers, lettuce and yoghurt are natural diuretics, thus helping reduce water retention.

- Tossing the apple slice with lemon juice prevents browning, which indicates oxidization of sugars.

TRICOLOUR SALAD
Tirangi Cholia Salaad

INGREDIENTS

2 cups / 20 gm Arugula / rocket
leaves (*salaad ke patte*)
½ cup / 65 gm Strawberry
½ cup / 80 gm Fresh green
chickpeas (*cholia*)
½ cup / 60 gm English
cucumber (*hara khira*), cut into
½-inch pieces

For the dressing:

1 tsp Extra virgin olive oil
1 tsp Honey
2 tsp Balsamic vinegar
⅛ tsp Salt
⅛ tsp freshly ground Black
peppercorn (*sabut kali mirch*)

METHOD

• Trim the stems of the salad leaves and tear any larger leaves into
half. Wash in plenty of cold water, drain in a colander and pat dry
with a kitchen towel. Set aside.

• Wash the strawberries and pat them dry with a kitchen towel.
Hull and slice them.

• Cover the chickpeas, strawberry slices, cucumber pieces and salad
leaves with cling film and refrigerate until chilled.

• Make the dressing by whisking together all the listed ingredients in
a bowl. Whisk well and set aside.

• **To serve**, place the salad leaves on a mixing plate and top
with the strawberry slices, fresh green chickpeas and chopped
cucumber.

• Drizzle the dressing over the salad. Toss gently, transfer to a
serving dish and serve immediately.

PER SERVING	1¾ CUP
Calories	97
Fat (grams)	3
Carbohydrates (grams)	13.5
Protein (grams)	4

• Salads make for excellent digestive aids as they are made from a
variety of water-rich and fibre-filled fruits and vegetables.

• This salad is packed with vitamin C, derived from the strawberries
and arugula.

WATER CHESTNUT SALAD
Singhara Khira Salaad

INGREDIENTS

3 cups / 60 gm Tropicana green leaf lettuce
15 Water chestnuts (*singhara*), peeled
1 cup / 120 gm English cucumber (*hara khira*), cut into 1-inch pieces
¾ cup / 120 gm Orange (*santra*), peeled to segments
1 Tbsp Peanuts (*moongphalli*), roasted, skinned (see pg. 211), to garnish

For the dressing:

1 tsp Honey
3 tsp Lemon (*nimbu*) juice
½ tsp *Chaat masala* (see pg. 222)
¼ tsp Salt

METHOD

- Tear the lettuce leaves roughly by hand into 2-inch pieces.

- In a bowl, cover the lettuce, water chestnuts, cucumber pieces and orange segments with cling film and refrigerate until chilled.

- Make the dressing by whisking together all the listed ingredients in a bowl.

- **To serve**, place the lettuce leaves on a serving plate. Arrange the water chestnuts, cucumber pieces and orange segments over the leaves.

- Drizzle the dressing over the salad. Toss gently, garnish with peanuts and serve chilled.

PER SERVING	2 CUPS
Calories	166.7
Fat (grams)	0.3
Carbohydrates (grams)	27.5
Protein (grams)	13.5

- The high-fibre water chestnut and the fluid-filled leafy lettuce make for a good combination to help clear one's digestive system.

- Oranges are an excellent source of potassium, which can help in rehydration.

SNACKS

MIXED LENTIL PANCAKE
Adai Dosa

INGREDIENTS

½ cup / 90 gm Small grain rice (*chote chawal*)

¼ cup / 45 gm De-husked, split Bengal gram (*chana dal*)

⅛ cup / 25 gm Yellow lentil (*arhar dal*)

⅛ cup / 25 gm De-husked, split black gram (*dhuli urad dal*)

⅛ cup / 25 gm Split green gram (*chilka moong dal*)

2 Tbsp Coconut (*nariyal*), grated (see pg. 210)

2 tsp Ginger (*adrak*), finely chopped

½ tsp Green chilli (*hari mirch*), chopped

2 Whole red chillies (*sabut lal mirch*)

⅛ tsp Asafoetida (*hing*)

1 tsp Fennel (*saunf*) seeds

Salt, to taste

1 Tbsp fresh Coriander (*dhaniya*) leaves, finely chopped

2 tsp Curry leaves (*kadhipatta*), finely chopped

5 tsp Rice bran oil

METHOD

• Soak the small grain rice, split Bengal gram, yellow lentil, split black gram and split green gram lentil in water for 4 hours. Drain into a colander and set aside.

• In a mixer, grind the soaked lentils with the coconut, ginger, green chillies and whole red chilli with a little water to a slightly coarse batter. Transfer the batter into a bowl.

• Add the asafoetida, fennel seeds, salt, chopped coriander and curry leaves. Mix well.

• Heat a non-stick pan for one minute over medium heat. Brush with a drop of oil, sprinkle a little water and wipe it off. Pour 1½ Tbsp of the batter in the centre of the pan and immediately spread the batter in a circular motion with the back of a flat spoon to a pancake of 6-inch diameter. Drizzle ½ tsp oil around the sides of the pancake and cook until the edges turn light golden brown. Flip and cook for 30 seconds. Flip again and fold.

• Repeat the same process with the remaining batter. Serve hot with Tomato Relish (see pg. 186).

PER SERVING	2 PANCAKES
Calories	270
Fat (grams)	2
Carbohydrates (grams)	11
Protein (grams)	2

• This is an ideal protein-packed snack for any time of the day.
• The batter can be refrigerated for up to 2 days.

• Rice bran oil has an ideal balance of heart-healthy fats – polyunsaturated fats and monounsaturated fats.

PEARL MILLET PANCAKES
Bajra Uttapam

INGREDIENTS

7 Tbsp levelled / 70 gm Pearl millet (*bajra*) flour
Salt, to taste
½ cup / 100 ml Water
¼ tsp Fruit salt
Pinch, Asafoetida (*hing*)
2 tsp Ginger (*adrak*) paste (see pg. 212)
½ tsp Green chilli (*hari mirch*) paste (see pg. 212)
½ cup / 75 gm Carrot (*gajar*), finely chopped
½ cup / 45 gm Cabbage (*patta gobhi*), finely chopped
1 Tbsp fresh Coriander (*dhaniya*) leaves, finely chopped
2 tsp Rice bran oil

METHOD

• In a medium-size bowl, add pearl millet flour, salt and water to prepare a semi-thick batter.

• Add the fruit salt, asafoetida, ginger, paste, green chilli paste, carrot, cabbage and coriander. Mix well and set aside.

• Heat a non-stick pan over medium heat for 30 seconds. Add ½ Tbsp batter and spread until 2 inches wide. Drizzle a little oil on the edges of the pancake. Cook until the edges begin to brown. Flip and cook for another 30 seconds. Flip again, remove and serve hot with Fresh Mint Yoghurt (see pg. 175).

PER SERVING	5 SMALL PANCAKES
Calories	206
Fat (grams)	7
Carbohydrates (grams)	255
Protein (grams)	4

• High protein and iron content can make *bajra* a little difficult to digest. Pairing it with yoghurt, which contains natural probiotics, is always beneficial.

SPROUTED BLACK CHICKPEA DELICACY
Ankurit Chana Chaat

INGREDIENTS

1 cup / 120 gm Black chickpea sprouts (*ankurit kala channa*) (see pg. 217)

1¼ cup / 112.5 gm Broccoli florets, cut into ½-inch florets

3 tsp Lemon (*nimbu*) juice

¼ tsp *Chaat masala* (see pg. 222)

¼ tsp Salt

2 tsp Ginger (*adrak*), finely chopped

¼ tsp Green chillies (*hari mirch*), finely chopped

½ cup / 62.5 gm Yellow bell pepper (*pili Shimla mirch*), cut into medium squares

½ cup / 62.5 gm Red bell pepper (*lal Shimla mirch*), cut into medium squares

2 Tbsp fresh Coriander (*dhaniya*) leaves, finely chopped

METHOD

- Steam the sprouted black chickpeas in a double boiler / vegetable steamer for 3 minutes (see pgs. 218–19). Remove and set aside to cool.

- Steam the broccoli florets for 2 minutes (see pgs. 218–19). Set aside to cool.

- In a small bowl, mix the lemon juice, *chaat masala* and salt. Set aside.

- **To serve**, in a mixing plate, add the sprouts, ginger, green chillies, broccoli, yellow and red bell pepper squares and coriander. Drizzle the lemon-*chaat masala* mixture over the vegetables and mix gently.

- Transfer to a serving bowl and serve immediately.

PER SERVING	1 cup
Calories	100.5
Fat (grams)	2.5
Carbohydrates (grams)	16
Protein (grams)	3.5

- Sprouted beans and whole lentils have higher levels of iron content.
- Vitamin C from the red and yellow bell peppers helps increase the absorption of iron.

- Black chickpeas generally take 2–3 days to sprout, and can take longer during the winter months.

TEA TIME TREAT
Chana Murmura

Serves: 4 (3 cups)
Suggested portion per serving: ¾ cup

PER SERVING	¾ CUP
Calories	181
Fat (grams)	5
Carbohydrates (grams)	26
Protein (grams)	8

INGREDIENTS

3 tsp Mustard oil (*sarson ka tel*)
25–30 Curry leaves (*kadhipatta*)
1 cup / 100 gm Roasted chickpeas (*bhuna chana*), skinned
2¼ cups / 40 gm Puffed rice (*murmura*)
⅛ tsp Salt
¼ tsp *Chaat masala* (see pg. 222)

METHOD

• Heat the oil in a broad pan for 30 seconds over medium heat. Add the curry leaves and roasted chickpeas and sauté for a minute. Add the puffed rice and salt. Mix and roast over low heat, stirring often for 10–15 minutes or until the puffed rice becomes crisp.

• Sprinkle the *chaat masala* and mix well.

• Cool to room temperature and serve.

• Roasted chickpeas and puffed rice make for a perfect protein and carbohydrate snack.

• If you plan to store this snack, cool it completely and then store in a dry, air-tight container. It may become moist if stored while warm.

BUCKWHEAT PANCAKES
Kuttu Ka Cheela

INGREDIENTS

100 gm Buckwheat (*kuttu*) flour
¾ cup + 1 tbsp / 165 ml Water
¼ tsp Salt
3 tsp Rice bran oil
1 cup / 200 gm low-fat Yoghurt
(*dahi*), as accompaniment

For the stuffing:

¾ cup / 50 gm Spinach (*palak*),
finely chopped (⅛ cup for each
pancake)
45 gm low-fat Cottage cheese
(*paneer*), grated (see pg. 206)
(7.5 gm for each pancake)

METHOD

• In a medium-size bowl, mix the buckwheat flour and water, adding the water gradually. Stir constantly to prepare a thin batter. Add salt and mix well.

• Heat a flat, 12-inch, non-stick griddle (*tawa*) for one minute over medium heat. Sprinkle a little water and wipe off with a kitchen towel.

• Pour 2 Tbsp of batter in the middle of the griddle. Immediately spread the batter in a circular motion with a small, flat-bottomed steel bowl (or the back of a tablespoon) to a create a pancake of 8-inch diameter.

• Drizzle ½ tsp of oil all around the pancake and cook over high heat until the pancake edges begin to turn a light golden brown. Flip the pancake and cook for 30 seconds. Flip again and place spinach and cottage cheese on one side of the pancake.

• Fold the pancake over the filling and serve hot with yoghurt.

PER SERVING	2 PANCAKES
Calories	114
Fat (grams)	6
Carbohydrates (grams)	12
Protein (grams)	3

• This recipe offers protein from the cottage cheese, iron from the spinach and essential vitamin B12 from the buckwheat.

• You can flavour the yoghurt with a pinch of salt, roasted cumin powder and fresh coriander.

ROASTED FEAST
Farsan

INGREDIENTS

1 cup / 15 gm Fox nuts
(*makkhana*)
1 tsp (¼ + ¾) Rice bran oil
½ cup / 75 gm Peanuts
(*moongphalli*)
3 Tbsp / 33 gm Amaranth
(*ramdana*) seeds
20 Sweet basil leaves
¼ tsp Salt
¼ tsp freshly ground Black
peppercorn (*sabut kali mirch*)
½ tsp Oregano powder

METHOD

- **To prepare the fox nuts**, remove any black outer shell on the fox nuts and discard. Place the fox nuts in a single layer on a baking tray. Brush the fox nuts with ¼ tsp of oil and bake in a pre-heated oven at 150°C for about 8–12 minutes, or until they become a light, toasted colour. Remove and set aside.

- **To roast the peanuts**, place the peanuts in a single layer on a baking tray and roast in a pre-heated oven at 180°C for 3–4 minutes or until they are light brown. Remove and set aside.

- **To prepare the amaranth seeds**, heat a broad pan over high heat until very hot. Add 1 tsp of amaranth seeds and swirl the seeds in the pan until they pop. Repeat the process to roast the remaining seeds in batches (see pg. 211). Sieve the roasted seeds, discarding the ones that have not popped.

- Heat the remaining ¾ tsp of oil in a broad pan for 30 seconds over medium heat. Add the basil leaves and sauté for 10 seconds.

- Now add the roasted peanuts, fox nuts, amaranth seeds, salt, black pepper and dried oregano. Mix well. Remove and set aside to cool completely. Serve.

- This snack can be stored in an air-tight jar for 1–2 days.

PER SERVING	1¼ CUP
Calories	281
Fat (grams)	17
Carbohydrates (grams)	21
Protein (grams)	9

- Fox nuts and amaranth are both good sources of iron, which helps in forming haemoglobin, the energy-providing component of red blood cells.

- Amaranth will puff up properly on a well-heated pan.

TANGY BEAN SPROUTS
Chatpati Ankurit Moong

PER SERVING	1 CUP
Calories	32
Fat (grams)	0
Carbohydrates (grams)	6
Protein (grams)	2

INGREDIENTS
1½ cups / 97.5 gm Whole green gram lentil (*sabut moong dal*) sprouts (see pg. 217)
½ cup / 60 gm English cucumber (*hara khira*), cut into medium-size cubes
½ cup / 75 gm Tomato (*tamatar*), cut into medium-size cubes (see pg. 224)
2 tsp Ginger (*adrak*), finely chopped
¼ tsp Green chillies (*hari mirch*), finely chopped
¼ tsp *Chaat masala* (see pg. 222)
1½ tsp Lemon (*nimbu*) juice
Salt, to taste
1 Tbsp fresh Coriander (*dhaniya*) leaves, finely chopped
A sprig of coriander, to garnish
2 Lemon slices, to garnish

METHOD
• Steam the bean sprouts in a double boiler / vegetable steamer for a minute over medium heat (see pgs. 218–19). Remove and set aside to cool.

• **To serve**, place the steamed sprouts with the cucumber, tomatoes, ginger, green chillies, *chaat masala*, lemon juice, salt and coriander in a mixing plate. Toss gently. Serve, garnished with a sprig of coriander and a couple of lemon slices.

• Sprouting beans and lentils increases its iron content.

• For those with digestive disorders, remove the seeds of cucumber to allow for easier digestion.

QUINOA PORRIDGE
Quinoa Daliya

INGREDIENTS
½ cup / 80 gm Quinoa
1¾ cups / 375 ml (¾ + 1) Water
2 cups / 400 ml Almond milk (*badam doodh*) (see pg. 226)
2 Tbsp Dates (*khajoor*), chopped (see pg. 209)
¼ tsp Green cardamom (*choti elaichi*) powder (see pg. 209)
2 Tbsp Honey
12 Almonds (*badam*), each cut into 3 pieces (see pg. 208), to garnish

METHOD
• Wash and soak the quinoa in water for 30 minutes. Drain and set aside.

• In a pan over medium heat, add ¾ cup / 175 ml of water and bring it to a boil. Add the soaked quinoa. Reduce the heat; cover and cook for 15–20 minutes, or until the water evaporates completely (see pg. 221).

• Add the almond milk and the remaining 1 cup / 200 ml of water. Bring to a boil and simmer for 5 minutes.

• Add the chopped dates, cardamom powder and honey. Mix well.

• Garnish with almonds and serve hot.

PER SERVING	²/₃ CUP
Calories	186
Fat (grams)	6
Carbohydrates (grams)	27
Protein (grams)	6

• Look for good-quality dates that are dried on iron plates, making them a good source of iron.

• Almond milk is naturally lactose-free, making it an ideal alternative for those who are lactose intolerant.

GREEN BANANA CUTLETS
Kache Kele Ki Tikki

INGREDIENTS

2 Tbsp / 20 gm levelled Flax seeds (*alsi ke beej*)

2 medium / 225 gm Green bananas (*kache kele*)

1½ cups / 300 ml Water

¼ tsp Salt

2 Tbsp fresh Coriander (*dhaniya*) leaves, finely chopped

For the stuffing:

125 gm Homemade cottage cheese (*paneer*), grated (see pg. 206)

1 tsp Ginger (*adrak*) paste (see pg. 212)

½ tsp Green chilli (*hari mirch*) paste (see pg. 212)

2 tsp fresh Coriander leaves, finely chopped

1/8 tsp Salt

2 tsp Rice bran oil

METHOD

• Grind the flax seeds to fine powder in a mixer. Remove and set aside.

• Wash the green bananas with the skin on. Place them on a cooking rack in a pressure cooker with water. Pressure cook over high heat to one whistle. Simmer for 8 minutes (see pg. 213). Turn off the heat, and once the pressure settles, remove the bananas. Peel and grate while they are hot.

• Mash the grated bananas well and add the ground flax seeds, salt and fresh coriander. Mix well and divide the mixture into 8 equal-sized balls.

• Mash the cottage cheese to a smooth paste (see pg. 206). Add the ginger and green chilli pastes, fresh coriander and salt. Mix well. Divide into 8 equal-sized balls and set aside.

• Dampen your palm with a little water and place a banana ball on it. Gently flatten the ball to a disc, about 2-inch in size. Place a ball of the cottage cheese mixture in the middle of the disc and carefully fold over, enclosing the cottage cheese filling inside. Gently flatten with your palm to shape into a cutlet.

• Heat a non-stick pan for a minute over medium heat and brush with 1 tsp oil. Place the cutlets, evenly-spaced, out on the pan and brush each one with the remaining 1 tsp of oil. Pan fry over low heat until golden brown on both sides, turning at regular intervals. While frying, gently press each cutlet with a flat spatula to ensure it cooks through. Serve hot with Green Gooseberry Chutney (see pg. 178).

PER SERVING	2 CUTLETS
Calories	171
Fat (grams)	7
Carbohydrates (grams)	19
Protein (grams)	8

• Green bananas are a good source of fibre and potassium, making this an ideal snack before a workout.

• It is important to grind the flax seeds down to a powder for maximizing their antioxidant and anti-carcinogenic properties.

ZESTY LOTUS STEM TREAT
Kamal Kakdi Ki Chaat

INGREDIENTS

½ cup / 100 gm Kidney beans (*rajma*), rinsed and soaked in water for 10 hours, drained
2½ cups / 500 ml (1 + 1½) Water
200 gm Lotus stem (*kamal kakdi*), peeled and cut into ¼-inch slant pieces
2 tsp Rice bran oil
1¼ cup / 250 gm low-fat Yoghurt (*dahi*)
½ tsp Salt
½ cup Green Gooseberry Chutney (see pg. 178)
5 tsp Tangy Date Chutney (see pg. 188)
¾ tsp roasted Cumin (*bhuna jeera*) powder (see pg. 222)
½ tsp Red chilli (*lal mirch*) powder
2 Tbsp fresh Coriander (*dhaniya*), finely chopped, to garnish

METHOD

- Pressure cook the soaked kidney beans with 1 cup / 200 ml water and ¼ tsp salt over high heat to one whistle and simmer for 15 minutes. Once the pressure settles, transfer the beans along with the water to a large, broad pan. Cook over high heat until the water evaporates. Remove and set aside.

- Place the lotus stem pieces in a small colander that fits into a pressure cooker. Set aside.

- Add 1½ cups / 300 ml of water to the pressure cooker. Place a cooking rack inside the pressure cooker. Place the colander with the lotus stem pieces on top of the cooking rack. Pressure cook over high heat to one whistle. Turn off the heat and let the pressure settle (see pg. 213). Remove the lotus stem pieces and set aside.

- Heat a griddle (*tawa*) for a minute over medium heat and brush with 1 tsp oil. Place the lotus stem pieces on the griddle and brush them with the remaining 1 tsp oil. Pan fry the lotus stem pieces for 1½ minutes on each side. Remove and set aside to cool.

- Whisk the yoghurt along with ¼ tsp salt and set aside.

- **To serve**, divide the lotus stem and kidney beans into five equal portions. Arrange one portion of lotus stem on a serving plate and one portion of the kidney beans on top of the lotus stem. Add 2 tsp Green Gooseberry Chutney, 2 Tbsp whisked yoghurt and 1 tsp Tangy Date Chutney. Sprinkle a little cumin powder and red chilli powder. Repeat to assemble the other portions. Garnish with coriander and serve.

PER SERVING	¾ CUP
Calories	135
Fat (grams)	3
Carbohydrates (grams)	21
Protein (grams)	6

- Lotus stem is a great source of fibre, making this a perfect recipe for maintaining blood sugar levels and lowering cholesterol levels.

- The seasoning of cumin and red chilli powder aids in digestion.

LENTIL PANCAKES
Dal Aur Methi Ka Chilla

INGREDIENTS

¾ cup / 150 gm Skinned, split green gram (*dhuli moong dal*), rinsed, soaked for 3 hours, drained

2 Tbsp / 30 gm De-husked, split Bengal gram (*chana dal*), rinsed, soaked for 3 hours, drained

2 tsp Ginger (*adrak*), finely chopped

1 tsp Green chillies (*hari mirch*), finely chopped

2 cups / 100 gm tightly packed Fenugreek (*methi*) leaves, washed, dried over a kitchen towel and finely chopped (see pg. 216)

Pinch, Asafoetida (*hing*)

⅛ tsp Carom (*ajwain*) seeds

¼ tsp Red chilli (*lal mirch*) powder

Salt, to taste

5 tsp Mustard oil (*sarson ka tel*)

METHOD

- Grind the soaked green gram, Bengal gram lentils, chopped ginger, green chillies and a little water to a smooth batter in a mixer. Add the chopped fenugreek leaves and pulse a couple of times to shred the leaves. Transfer the batter to a bowl.

- Add the asafoetida, carom seeds and red chilli powder. Season to taste with salt. Mix well and set aside.

- Heat a non-stick pan for one minute over medium heat, brush with a little oil and wipe it off. Pour 1½ Tbsp of the batter in the centre of the pan and immediately spread the batter in a circular motion with the back of a flat spoon to create a pancake of 5-inch diameter. Drizzle ½ tsp oil around the sides of the pancake and cook until the edges appear light golden brown. Flip and cook for 30 seconds. Flip again and fold.

- Serve hot with Green Gooseberry Chutney (see pg. 178) and Tangy Date Chutney (see pg. 188).

PER SERVING	2 PANCAKES
Calories	156
Fat (grams)	4
Carbohydrates (grams)	21
Protein (grams)	9

- Fresh fenugreek leaves are a good source of calcium.

- Lentils are a good source of protein, but are generally heavy on the stomach. Adding carom seeds and asafoetida aids in proper digestion of the lentils.

FENUGREEK SAVOURY CAKE
Methi Muthia

INGREDIENTS

1½ cups / 150 gm Black gram flour (*kaale channe ka atta*), sieved
Pinch, Asafoetida (*hing*)
1¼ tsp Fruit salt
⅛ tsp Turmeric (*haldi*) powder
½ tsp Salt
1½ cups / 250 gm Bottle gourd (*lauki*), peeled and grated
2 cups / 100 gm tightly packed Fenugreek (*methi*) leaves, washed, dried on kitchen towel, finely chopped (see pg. 216)
2 tsp Ginger (*adrak*) paste (see pg. 212)
1 tsp Green chilli (*hari mirch*) paste (see pg. 212)
3½ tsp (½ + 1 + 1 + 1) Rice bran oil
¼ tsp Carom (*ajwain*) seeds
2 Tbsp fresh Coconut (*nariyal*), grated (see pg. 210), to garnish
2 Tbsp fresh Coriander (*dhaniya*) leaves, finely chopped, to garnish

For the tempering:
2 tsp Rice bran oil
¼ tsp Mustard (*sarson*) seeds
20 Curry leaves (*kadhipatta*)

METHOD

• In a mixing plate, mix the gram flour with asafoetida, fruit salt, turmeric powder and salt. Add the grated bottle gourd, fenugreek leaves, ginger and green chilli pastes. Knead together with a little water to make a dough that is firm, but not soft. Divide the dough into 3 equal portions.

• Shape each portion into a cylinder that is 2 inches thick.

• Brush ½ tsp oil on a flat mesh. Place the cylinders on the mesh and steam for 25–30 minutes in a vegetable steamer / double boiler. To check if the savoury cakes are cooked, gently pierce with a cooking needle / toothpick; it should come out clean. Remove and set aside to cool completely.

• Slice the cylinders to make 25 savoury cakes / *muthia*.

• Heat a non-stick pan for a minute over medium heat and brush with ½ tsp oil. Arrange a few of the savoury cakes in the pan and brush with another ½ tsp oil on top. Pan fry the savoury cakes until light brown on both sides. Repeat the process in two more batches with the remaining savoury cakes (using 1 tsp oil per batch). Transfer to a serving plate.

• **For the tempering,** heat 2 tsp of oil in a tempering ladle for 30 seconds. Add the mustard seeds, and when they splutter, add the curry leaves. Pour the tempering over the savoury cakes and serve with Green Gooseberry Chutney (see pg. 178).

• Garnish with grated fresh coconut and coriander.

PER SERVING	5 PIECES
Calories	133
Fat (grams)	5
Carbohydrates (grams)	15
Protein (grams)	7

• Adding vegetables to your teatime snack packs in vitamins, minerals and fibre, helping in weight management.

• Black gram flour may be difficult to digest. Adding fruit salt helps to lighten the dough.

FINGER MILLET RICE CAKE
Ragi Idli

INGREDIENTS

2 cups / 420 gm Fermented rice cake (*idli*) batter (see pg. 227)
¼ tsp Salt
2 Tbsp Finger millet (*ragi*) flour
1 tsp Rice bran oil

METHOD

- In a mixing bowl, add the fermented rice cake batter and season to taste with salt. Add the finger millet flour and mix well. Grease the rice cake / *idli* stand with 1 tsp oil.

- Spoon 1½ Tbsp of batter into each mould.

- Heat a double boiler, place the rice cake stand inside and steam for 8–10 minutes. To check if it is done, pierce one of the rice cakes with a cooking needle / toothpick; it should come out clean.

- With a sharp knife, loosen the edges of the rice cake and unmould carefully. Turn it over so that the curved surface faces upwards. Serve hot with Lentil Stew (see pg. 128) and Roasted Peanut Chutney (see pg. 179).

PER SERVING	2 RICE CAKES
Calories	107
Fat (grams)	3
Carbohydrates (grams)	17
Protein (grams)	3

- Ragi contains essential amino acids, which are the building blocks of protein.

- The combination of complex carbohydrates from the rice and protein from the finger millet makes this a wholesome snack.

FINGER MILLET PANCAKE
Ragi Dosa

INGREDIENTS

¼ cup / 50 gm De-husked, split black gram (*dhuli urad dal*)

½ tsp Fenugreek seeds (*methi dana*)

½ cup / 100 ml Water

1 cup / 125 gm Finger millet (*ragi*) flour

½ tsp Salt

8 tsp Rice bran oil (½ tsp per pancake / *dosa*)

METHOD

- In a bowl, mix the split black gram with the fenugreek seeds. Wash well and soak in water for 8 hours.

- Grind this mixture with the water to a smooth batter in a mixer. Transfer to a broad vessel.

- Add the finger millet flour and salt to this batter and mix well. If required, add a little more water to make a semi-thick batter. Cover and allow the batter to ferment overnight or for 10 hours, and set aside.

- Heat a non-stick griddle (*tawa*) for a minute over medium heat. Brush the griddle with a little oil, sprinkle a few drops of water and wipe off with a kitchen towel.

- Pour 1 Tbsp of the batter in the middle of the griddle. Using the back of a rounded spoon, spread the batter in a circular motion to create a pancake of 5 inches in diameter. Drizzle ½ tsp of oil around the edges. Cook the pancake / *dosa* until the edges begin to brown, flip and cook for a further 20 seconds. Flip again, fold and serve hot with Tomato Relish (see pg. 186).

PER SERVING	2 SMALL PANCAKES
Calories	75
Fat (grams)	3
Carbohydrates (grams)	11
Protein (grams)	1

- This is a protein-packed recipe thanks to the split black gram and the finger millet flour.

- Finger millet is a good source of iron when paired with vitamin C from the Tomato Relish, which helps absorption of the iron from the pancake.

SAVOURY FLATTENED RED RICE
Lal Poha

INGREDIENTS

1 cup / 80 gm Flattened red rice (*lal chiwda*)
5 cups / 1 L Water
2 tsp Rice bran oil
¼ tsp Mustard (*sarson*) seeds
2 tsp Ginger (*adrak*), finely chopped
1 slit Green chilli (*hari mirch*)
15 Curry leaves (*kadhipatta*)
3 cups / 270 gm Broccoli florets, cut into ½-inch pieces
Salt, to taste
2 tsp Lemon (*nimbu*) juice
2 Tbsp fresh Coriander (*dhaniya*) leaves, finely chopped
1 Tbsp Peanuts (*moongphalli*) roasted, skinned (see pg. 211), to garnish

METHOD

- Soak the flattened rice in water for 30 seconds. Drain in a colander. Set aside.

- Heat the oil in a broad pan for 30 seconds over medium heat. Add the mustard seeds. Cook until the seeds begin to crackle. Add the ginger, green chilli and curry leaves; mix. Add the broccoli florets and mix again.

- Now add 2 Tbsp water and cook until the moisture evaporates, stirring occasionally.

- Reduce the heat and add the flattened rice; mix gently. Add the salt, lemon juice and fresh coriander. Mix well. Cook over high heat for a minute, mixing occasionally.

- Serve hot, garnished with peanuts.

PER SERVING	¾ CUP
Calories	121
Fat (grams)	4.5
Carbohydrates (grams)	15
Protein (grams)	5

- Flattened red rice contains more fibre and trace minerals than regular flattened white rice.

- Flattened rice needs a gentle wash, so don't soak for longer than mentioned. It will become soggy.

MIXED VEGETABLE QUINOA
Sabz Quinoa

INGREDIENTS

½ cup / 80 gm Quinoa
¾ cup / 150 ml Water
¾ cup / 105 gm Carrot (*gajar*),
cut into medium cubes
¾ cup / 60 gm Haricot beans,
cut into thin slices (see pg. 214)
2 tsp Rice bran oil
¼ tsp Mustard (*sarson*) seeds
2 tsp Ginger (*adrak*), finely
chopped
15 Curry leaves (*kadhipatta*)
½ cup / 60 gm Onion (*pyaz*),
cut into medium cubes (see
pg. 215)
⅛ tsp Turmeric (*haldi*) powder
½ cup / 75 gm Tomatoes
(*tamatar*), cut into medium
cubes (see pg. 224)
¼ tsp Red chilli (*lal mirch*)
powder
Salt, to taste
2 tsp Lemon (*nimbu*) juice
2 Tbsp fresh Coriander
(*dhaniya*) leaves, finely chopped
Sprigs of coriander, to garnish

PER SERVING	1 CUP
Calories	160
Fat (grams)	4
Carbohydrates (grams)	25
Protein (grams)	6

METHOD

• Wash and soak quinoa in
water for 30 minutes. Drain
and set aside.

• Boil ¾ cup / 150 ml of water
in a pan and add the soaked
quinoa. Bring to a boil, cover
and cook over low heat for
15–20 minutes, or until the
water evaporates completely.

• Steam carrots and beans
together in a double boiler /

vegetable steamer over
medium heat for two minutes
(see pgs. 218–19). Remove
and set aside.

• Heat oil in a pan for 30
seconds over medium heat.
Add the mustard seeds.
Cook until the seeds begin to
crackle. Add the ginger and
curry leaves; mix and sauté
for 10 seconds.

• Add the onion and sauté for
30 seconds. Add the steamed
beans and carrots, mix well
and cook for one minute. Add
the turmeric powder and mix.

• Now add the cooked quinoa,
tomatoes, red chilli powder,
salt to taste, lemon juice and
the fresh coriander leaves and
mix well.

• Serve hot, garnished with a
few sprigs of coriander.

• Quinoa is a good source of protein for vegetarians. It is available
in three colours – white, red and black. You may use any one for
this recipe.

RICE NOODLES WITH BEAN SPROUTS
Chawal Ki Sewai Aur Ankurit Moong

INGREDIENTS

3½ cups / 700 ml Water
50 gm Rice noodles
2 cups / 130 gm Whole green gram sprouts (*ankurit sabut moong*) (see pg. 217)
1¼ cup / 140 gm Carrot (*gajar*) julienne (see pg. 214)
¾ cup / 60 gm Haricot beans, cut into thin, slant slices (see pg. 214)
2 tsp De-husked, split black gram (*dhuli urad dal*)
2 tsp De-husked, split Bengal gram (*chana dal*)
2 tsp Rice bran oil
¼ tsp Mustard (*sarson*) seeds
2 tsp Ginger (*adrak*), finely chopped
½ tsp Green chilli (*hari mirch*), finely chopped
15 Curry leaves (*kadhipatta*)
Salt, to taste
2 tsp Lemon (*nimbu*) juice
2 Tbsp fresh Coriander (*dhaniya*) leaves, finely chopped

METHOD

• In a broad pan over medium heat, bring the water to a boil. Add the rice noodles and turn the heat off immediately. Cover the pan and allow the noodles to cook in the hot water for 2 minutes. Drain the noodles in a colander and cut into smaller pieces with a pair of scissors. Set aside.

• Steam the bean sprouts, carrot julienne and sliced haricot beans for a minute in a vegetable steamer / double boiler (see pgs. 218–19). Remove and set aside.

• Mix the split black gram and the split Bengal gram. Wash well, drain in a colander and set aside.

• Heat 2 tsp of oil in a broad pan for 30 seconds over medium heat. Add the lentils and fry for 30 seconds. Add the mustard seeds. Cook until the seeds begin to crackle, and add the chopped ginger, green chillies and curry leaves. Mix well.

• Add the steamed vegetables and sprouts; mix and cook for a minute. Add the rice noodles, salt and lemon juice; toss gently with a fork and cook for a minute. Add the fresh coriander and toss again. Serve hot.

PER SERVING	1½ CUP
Calories	136
Fat (grams)	4
Carbohydrates (grams)	21
Protein (grams)	4

• Rice noodles are complex carbohydrates, which, along with the variety of vegetables in this recipe, help maintain blood sugar levels.

• With almost all food groups covered in this recipe – starch, sprouts, vegetables and oil for cooking – this snack can also double up as a mini-meal.

ROASTED RICE CAKE
Paniharan

INGREDIENTS

2 Tbsp / 20 gm Flax seeds
(*alsi ke beej*)
2 cups / 240 gm Fermented
steamed rice cake (*idli*) batter
(see pg. 227)
¾ cup / 90 gm Onions (*pyaz*),
finely chopped (see pg. 215)
2 tsp Ginger (*adrak*) paste (see
pg. 212)
¼ tsp Green chilli (*hari mirch*)
paste (see pg. 212)
¼ tsp Salt
2 Tbsp fresh Coriander
(*dhaniya*) leaves, finely chopped
3 tsp Rice bran oil

METHOD

• In a mixer, grind the flax seeds into a fine powder.

• Mix the rice cake / *idli* batter with the flax seed powder, chopped onion, ginger and green chilli pastes, salt and fresh coriander leaves. Mix well, set aside.

• Heat the pancake puff pan for a minute over medium heat. Brush the mould with 1 tsp oil.

• Pour 1½ tsp of batter into each mould and cover with a lid. Cook over medium-high heat until the edges begin to brown.

• Flip and cook for a minute, or until cooked through. Repeat the same process with the remaining batter.

• Remove and serve hot with Lentil Stew (see pg. 128) or Yoghurt-Mustard Sauce (see pg. 181).

PER SERVING	5 PIECES
Calories	100
Fat (grams)	4
Carbohydrates (grams)	12
Protein (grams)	4

• Choose steamed snacks versus fried. Steaming helps keep nutritional values intact and keeps a check on calories.

• Flax seeds are a good source of alpha linolenic acid, an omega 3 fatty acid shown to help reduce the risk of heart disease.

BARNYARD MILLET FEAST
Samvat Upma

INGREDIENTS

¼ cup / 50 gm Barnyard millet
(*samvat ke chawal*)
3¾ cups / 750 ml Water
3 tsp (1+ 2) Rice bran oil
1 tsp De-husked, split black
gram (*dhuli urad dal*)
1 tsp De-husked, split Bengal
gram (*chana dal*)
½ tsp Mustard (*sarson*) seeds
15 Curry leaves (*kadhipatta*)
¾ cup / 90 gm Onion (*pyaz*),
cut into medium cubes
2 tsp Ginger (*adrak*) chopped
1½ cup / 150 gm Green bell
pepper (*shimla mirch*), cut into
medium cubes
Salt, to taste
1 slit Green chilli (*hari mirch*)
2 Tbsp fresh Coriander
(*dhaniya*) leaves, finely chopped
2 Tbsp Peanuts (*moongphalli*),
roasted, skinned (see pg. 211)

METHOD

- Rinse and soak barnyard millet in water for 15 minutes; drain
  and set aside. In a pan over medium heat, take 3¾ cups / 750 ml
  water and bring it to a boil. Add the soaked barnyard millet and
  cook for a minute. Immediately drain using a micro sieve. Add
  1 tsp oil and keep mixing gently until the millet cools at room
  temperature (see pg. 221).

- Mix both the lentils together. Wash well with water, drain in a
  colander and set aside.

- Heat 2 tsp oil in a broad pan for 30 seconds over medium heat,
  and add the mustard seeds, curry leaves and soaked lentils. Cook
  for 10 seconds. Add onion and ginger and cook for 30 seconds,
  stirring frequently. Add green bell pepper and cook for 30 seconds,
  mixing occasionally. Add the cooked barnyard millet, salt, slit green
  chilli, chopped coriander and peanuts. Mix gently and cook for a
  minute, stirring constantly, and serve hot.

PER SERVING	¾ CUP
Calories	157
Fat (grams)	9
Carbohydrates (grams)	16
Protein (grams)	4

- Barnyard millet has the lowest carbohydrate content amongst all the
  millets, making it a good option for weight management meal plans.

- Barnyard millet is also known as *saamai*, *samak* and *vari tandur*.

SAVOURY LENTIL CAKES
Moong Dal Dhokla

INGREDIENTS

¾ cup / 150 gm Skinned, split green gram (*dhuli moong dal*), rinsed, soaked in ¼ cup / 50 ml water for 3 hours, drained
4 cups / 800 ml Water
¼ tsp Sugar
1/8 tsp Turmeric (*haldi*) powder
¾ tsp Salt
¼ tsp Citric acid (*nimbu ka satt*)
¾ tsp Fruit salt
1 Tbsp Rice bran oil
½ tsp Mustard (*sarson*) seeds
4 slit Green chillies (*hari mirch*)
20 Curry leaves (*kadhipatta*)
¼ tsp Red chilli (*lal mirch*) powder, to garnish
1 Tbsp Fresh coriander (*dhaniya*) leaves, finely chopped, to garnish
1 Tbsp fresh Coconut (*nariyal*), grated (see pg. 210), to garnish

METHOD

- In a mixer, grind the green gram with ¼ cup / 50 ml water into a slightly coarse texture.

- In a double boiler containing 3¾ cups / 750 ml water, place a greased and round steel container.

- While the container is being heated, mix the green gram batter with sugar, turmeric powder, salt and citric acid. Add the fruit salt and keep stirring until the batter begins to fluff up.

- Carefully remove the heated container from the double boiler and pour the batter into the hot container.

- Place the container back into the double boiler, cover and steam over high heat for 10–12 minutes or until done. To check if the lentil cake / *dhokla* is cooked through, pierce with a toothpick; it should come out clean. Remove the container and evenly add 2–3 Tbsp of water over the steamed lentil cake. Set aside to cool.

- Loosen the sides of the cake with a sharp knife. Carefully remove the entire lentil cake from the container and place on a flat plate. Cut into 12 diagonal pieces.

- In a broad pan over medium heat, heat 1 Tbsp of oil for 30 seconds. Add the mustard seeds. Cook until the seeds begin to crackle. Add the slit green chillies and curry leaves; mix.

- Add the lentil cake / *dhokla* pieces. Garnish with red chilli powder, fresh coriander and grated fresh coconut. Mix gently.

- Serve hot, accompanied with Green Gooseberry Chutney (see pg. 178).

PER SERVING	2 PIECES
Calories	116
Fat (grams)	4
Carbohydrates (grams)	14
Protein (grams)	6

- These savoury lentil cakes are an ideal and fresh teatime snack that keeps the calories in control.

- Citric acid is a concentrate substitute of lemon juice, which enhances the perfect sourness needed in this recipe.

MAIN COURSE

BITTER GOURD WITH SPRING ONIONS
Hara Pyaz Ka Karela

INGREDIENTS

250 gm tender Bitter gourd
(karela)
½ tsp Salt
3 tsp (2 + 1) Mustard oil (sarson
ka tel)
2 cups / 100 gm loosely packed
Spring onion leaves (hara pyaz
ke patte), finely chopped (see
pg. 216)
½ cup / 55 gm Spring onion
(hara pyaz) bulb, cut into
long slices
¼ tsp Red chilli (lal mirch)
powder
1 tsp Fennel (sauf) powder
¼ tsp Mango powder (amchur)
Salt, to taste

METHOD

• Roughly peel the ridges off the bitter gourd and cut into ⅛-inch slant slices; sprinkle ½ tsp salt all over and set aside for 2 hours.

• Press the bitter gourd between your palms to squeeze out the liquid.

• Steam the bitter gourd in a double boiler / vegetable steamer for 4 minutes (see pgs. 218–19). Remove and set aside to cool.

• Heat a griddle (tawa) for 30 seconds over medium heat and brush with ½ tsp of mustard oil. Place half the bitter gourd pieces, brush with ½ tsp oil and roast on both sides until light golden brown. Remove, set aside. Repeat the same process to roast the remaining bitter gourd pieces using oil.

• In a broad pan over medium heat, heat 1 tsp oil for 30 seconds and add the onion slices. Sauté for 30 seconds; add the roasted bitter gourd, chilli powder, fennel powder, dry mango powder and salt to taste. Cook over medium heat for a minute, stirring continuously. Add the onion leaves and toss over medium heat for 20 seconds. Remove and serve hot.

PER SERVING	½ CUP
Calories	58
Fat (grams)	2
Carbohydrates (grams)	7
Protein (grams)	3

• The substantial amount of vitamin C in bitter gourd helps in absorbing its iron content.

• Squeezing bitter gourd after adding salt makes the vegetable less bitter.

- If the spring onions do not have well-formed white bulbs, substitute with regular onions.

CARROTS & FLAT GREEN BEANS
Gajar Aur Sem Phali

METHOD

- String the flat green beans, place them flat on the chopping board and cut them into thin pieces.

- Wash and peel the carrots. Cut the carrots into diagonal pieces of ¼-inch thickness. Cut each diagonal carrot piece into long, thin pieces (see pg. 214).

- In a broad pan over medium heat, heat the oil for 30 seconds. Add the asafoetida, cumin seeds, turmeric powder and chilli powders. Mix well.

- Add the flat green beans and carrots and mix gently. Lower the heat, add salt to taste and cover the pan. Cook for 2 minutes. Uncover and toss at frequent intervals, adjusting the heat between low and medium until the vegetables are tender but firm.

- Add the fresh coriander leaves, mix and serve.

PER SERVING	½ CUP
Calories	42
Fat (grams)	2
Carbohydrates (grams)	4
Protein (grams)	2

INGREDIENTS

250 gm Flat green beans
(sem phali)
2 medium / 150 gm Carrots
(gajar)
2 tsp Rice bran oil
Pinch, Asafoetida (hing)
½ tsp Cumin (jeera) seeds
1/8 tsp Turmeric (haldi) powder
1/8 tsp Red chilli (lal mirch)
powder
Salt, to taste
2 Tbsp fresh Coriander
(dhaniya) leaves, finely chopped

- Packed with vitamin A, the vegetables used in this recipe are anti-ageing and good for the eyes.

- Be careful while cooking flat beans. Overcooking may change them from bright green to a dull colour, indicating loss of nutritional value.

CARROTS WITH FENUGREEK LEAVES
Gajar Methi

INGREDIENTS

250 gm Red carrot (*gajar*)
4 cups / 200 gm tightly packed Fenugreek (*methi*) leaves, washed, dried over kitchen towel and finely chopped (see pg. 216)
2 tsp Rice bran oil
Pinch, Asafoetida (*hing*)
½ tsp Cumin (*jeera*) seeds
Salt, to taste
¼ tsp Red chilli (*lal mirch*) powder

PER SERVING	½ CUP
Calories	42
Fat (grams)	2
Carbohydrates (grams)	4
Protein (grams)	2

METHOD

- Wash and peel the carrots. Cut the carrots into diagonal pieces of ¼-inch thickness. Cut each diagonal carrot piece into thin, long slices (see pg. 214). Set aside.

- In a broad pan over medium heat, heat the oil for 30 seconds. Add asafoetida, cumin seeds, carrots and salt to taste. Cover and cook for 30 seconds. Lower the heat and continue cooking, stirring occasionally until the carrots are tender yet firm.

- Uncover the lid and add chilli powder. Stir gently over high heat. Add 2 cups of chopped fenugreek leaves and cook for 20 seconds, stirring constantly. Add the remaining fenugreek leaves, tossing constantly for another 20 seconds. Remove and serve hot.

- This recipe is packed with immunity-boosting properties with large amounts of the antioxidants vitamin A and C, ideal during pregnancy when immunity may be compromised.

- Red carrots can be substituted with orange carrots, which take a little longer to cook.

CLUSTER BEANS WITH FENUGREEK SPROUTS
Guar Phali Aur Methi

Serves: 3 (1½ cups)
Suggested portion per serving: ½ cup

PER SERVING	½ CUP
Calories	100
Fat (grams)	4
Carbohydrates (grams)	6
Protein (grams)	10

INGREDIENTS
250 gm Cluster beans
(*guar phali*)
3 tsp Mustard oil (*sarson ka tel*)
Pinch, Asafoetida (*hing*)
⅛ tsp Carom seeds (*ajwain*)
½ Red chilli (*lal mirch*) powder
2 tsp Coriander (*dhaniya*)
powder
⅛ tsp Mango powder (*amchur*)
Salt, to taste
¾ cup / 60 gm sprouted
Fenugreek (*methi*) (see pg. 217)

METHOD
- Wash the cluster beans and pat dry with a kitchen towel. String the beans and cut them into ½-inch pieces. Steam in a double boiler / vegetable steamer for 15 minutes (see pgs. 218–19). Set aside.

- In a broad pan over medium heat, heat 2 tsp mustard oil for 30 seconds. Add the asafoetida, carom seeds and steamed cluster beans. Mix well. Add the red chilli, coriander powder and mango powder. Season to taste with salt. Cook for a minute over low heat. Add the sprouted fenugreek; mix and cook for 30 seconds, stirring gently. Serve hot.

- Cluster beans have a high content of both iron and vitamin C, making it an ideal choice for anyone.

- The sprouted fenugreek adds extra iron to this recipe, making it nutritionally packed.

COASTAL RED AMARANTH
Lal Saag

Serves: 5 (2½ cups)
Suggested portion per serving: ½ cup

INGREDIENTS

500 gm Red amaranth leaves (*lal saag*)
2 tsp De-husked, split black gram (*dhuli urad dal*)
2 tsp De-husked, split Bengal gram (*chana dal*)
2 tsp Rice bran oil
Pinch, Asafoetida (*hing*)
¼ tsp Mustard (*sarson*) seeds
20 Curry leaves (*kadhipatta*)
2 tsp Ginger (*adrak*), slivered
2 Green chillies (*hari mirch*), slit
Salt, to taste
2 Tbsp fresh Coconut (*nariyal*), grated (see pg. 210), to garnish

METHOD

- Wash the amaranth leaves in water, drain in a colander and pat dry with a kitchen towel. Remove the threads of the amaranth stems.

- Finely chop the stems and the remaining amaranth leaves. Set aside.

- Mix both the lentils. Rinse well with water, drain in a colander and set aside.

- In a heavy-bottom vessel over medium heat, heat the oil for 30 seconds. Add the lentils and cook until they turn light brown in colour. Add the asafoetida, mustard seeds, curry leaves, ginger and green chillies. Mix well. Add the amaranth leaves, mix well and cook covered for 2 minutes.

- Uncover, add salt to taste and cook, stirring occasionally, until the water evaporates. Garnish with grated coconut and serve hot.

PER SERVING	½ CUP
Calories	92
Fat (grams)	4
Carbohydrates (grams)	9
Protein (grams)	5

- Red amaranth is a good source of several B vitamins. These vitamins help get energy out of foods so the body may utilize it.

- Red amaranth should be added to prenatal meal plans as it also provides folic acid, zinc and iron – all essential during pregnancy.

CURRIED BLACK-EYED PEAS
Rassedar Lobia

INGREDIENTS
¾ cup / 150 gm Black-eyed peas (*lobia*), rinsed, soaked for 4 hours in water and drained
2 cups / 400 ml Water
Salt, to taste
½ tsp (¼ + ¼) Turmeric (*haldi*) powder
2 tsp Rice bran oil
Pinch, Asafoetida (*hing*)
½ tsp Cumin (*jeera*) seeds
2 tsp Ginger (*adrak*), finely chopped
¼ tsp Green chillies (*hari mirch*), finely chopped
⅓ tsp Red chilli (*lal mirch*) powder
3 medium / 200 gm Tomatoes (*tamatar*), liquidized (see pg. 225)
2 Tbsp Coriander (*dhaniya*) leaves, finely chopped, to garnish

METHOD
- Pressure cook the soaked black-eyed peas with 2 cups / 400 ml water, ⅛ tsp salt and ¼ tsp turmeric powder to one whistle. Simmer for five minutes and turn off the heat. Wait until the pressure settles, remove the lid and set aside.

- In a broad pan over medium heat, heat the oil for 30 seconds. Add the asafoetida, cumin seeds, ginger, green chillies, red chilli powder, the remaining turmeric powder and liquidized tomatoes. Cook for 2 minutes, stirring occasionally.

- Add the pressure-cooked black-eyed peas along with the water they were cooked in. Season to taste with salt. Bring the mixture to a boil, lower the heat and simmer for 8–10 minutes.

- Garnish with the coriander leaves and serve hot.

PER SERVING	½ CUP
Calories	116
Fat (grams)	3
Carbohydrates (grams)	18.5
Protein (grams)	8.5

- Black-eyed peas are a good source of both protein and potassium. Try this dish after a strenuous workout to avoid muscle soreness and cramping.

FENUGREEK-FLAVOURED YELLOW LENTIL
Arhar Dal Aur Methi

Serves: 6 (3 cups)
Suggested portion per serving: ½ cup

PER SERVING	½ CUP
Calories	119
Fat (grams)	5
Carbohydrates (grams)	14.5
Protein (grams)	4

INGREDIENTS
1 cup / 50 gm tightly packed Fenugreek (*methi*) leaves, washed, dried over a kitchen towel and finely chopped (see pg. 216)
¾ cups / 150 gm Yellow lentil (*arhar dal*), rinsed, soaked in water for 30 minutes and drained
2¼ cup / 450 ml Water
⅓ tsp Turmeric (*haldi*) powder
Salt, to taste
2 tsp Ginger (*adrak*), finely chopped
1 Green chilli (*hari mirch*) slit
1 medium / 75 gm Tomato (*tamatar*), grated (see pg. 224)
1 medium / 75 gm Tomato, roasted, peeled, cut into cubes (see pg. 224)
For the tempering:
2 tsp Rice bran oil
Pinch, Asafoetida (*hing*)
½ tsp Cumin (*jeera*) seeds
¼ tsp Red chilli (*lal mirch*) powder

METHOD
• Heat a broad pan for 30 seconds over medium heat and add the fenugreek leaves. Cook covered for 10 seconds. Mix, remove and set aside.

• Pressure cook the soaked yellow lentil with 2¼ cups (450 ml) of water, turmeric powder and salt to taste for one whistle. Simmer for 5 minutes and turn off the heat. Wait until the pressure releases.

• Remove the lid and add the cooked fenugreek leaves, ginger, slit green chilli, grated tomato and roasted tomato cubes. Bring the mixture to a boil over medium heat. Transfer to a serving dish.

• **For the tempering,** heat the oil in a tempering ladle for 20 seconds over medium heat. Add the asafoetida, cumin seeds and red chilli powder, and immediately pour over the lentil. Serve hot.

• Lentils contain a significant amount of starch. Washing and soaking lentils can help remove some of the starchiness, making it a good protein option.

• To give a fresh look to the lentils, always add the tempering just before serving.

GINGER-FLAVOURED CAULIFLOWER
Adraki Gobhi

INGREDIENTS

500 gm Cauliflower (*phool gobi*), cut into 1½-inch florets (approximately 30 pieces)
2 tsp Rice bran oil
Pinch, Asafoetida (*hing*)
½ tsp Cumin (*jeera*) seeds
2 tsp Ginger (*adrak*), finely chopped
1 tsp Green chillies (*hari mirch*), finely chopped
¼ tsp Turmeric (*haldi*) powder
¼ tsp Red chilli (*lal mirch*) powder
⅓ cup / 65 ml Water
¼ tsp Spice mix (*garam masala*) (see pg. 222)
¼ tsp Mango powder (*amchur*)
2 Tbsp fresh Coriander (*dhaniya*) leaves, finely chopped

METHOD

- In a heavy-bottom vessel over medium heat, heat the oil for 30 seconds. Add the asafoetida, cumin seeds, ginger, green chillies, turmeric powder and red chilli powder. Mix well.

- Add the cauliflower pieces and salt to taste; mix. Add the water, cover and cook over medium heat, stirring occasionally, until the water dries and the pieces are tender but firm.

- Add the spice mix powder, mango powder and the fresh coriander leaves. Mix gently and serve.

PER SERVING	½ CUP
Calories	31
Fat (grams)	1
Carbohydrates (grams)	2.5
Protein (grams)	3

- Cauliflower is a good source of folate, which helps prevent neural tube defects in newborn babies, making it a good vegetable option for expecting mothers. Ginger also helps to alleviate morning sickness.

- In case the water dries up and the cauliflower is still not cooked, it is advised to cook for 2 more minutes, covered over low heat.

GRAVY-STYLE INDIAN BABY PUMPKIN
Rassedar Tinda

INGREDIENTS

250 gm Indian baby pumpkin (*tinda*)
2 tsp Rice bran oil
Pinch, Asafoetida (*hing*)
¼ tsp Cumin (*jeera*) seeds
¼ tsp Turmeric (*haldi*) powder
¼ tsp Red chilli (*lal mirch*) powder
1 ½ cups / 300 ml Water
Salt, to taste
1 ½ Tbsp Tomato (*tamatar*) masala (see pg. 225)
1 tsp Ginger (*adrak*), finely chopped
1 ½ Tbsp fresh Coriander (*dhaniya*) leaves, finely chopped

METHOD

• Scrape the pumpkin with the blunt side of a knife and slit into half. Cut each half vertically into ¼-inch-long slices. Set aside.

• Heat 2 tsp oil in a pan for 30 seconds over medium heat. Add asafoetida and cumin seeds. Lower the heat. Add turmeric, chilli powder and Indian baby pumpkin pieces; mix. Add 1 ½ cups (300 ml) water and salt to taste. Cook covered for 6 minutes. The pumpkin should be soft by this time. If not, cook covered for another two minutes over low heat.

• Add 1 ½ tsp tomato masala, mix and cook for one minute. Add chopped ginger and finely chopped coriander leaves. Serve hot.

PER SERVING	½ CUP
Calories	67
Fat (grams)	3
Carbohydrates (grams)	7.5
Protein (grams)	2.5

• Indian baby pumpkins are a low-calorie vegetable with high water content, which helps alleviate acidity and constipation.

• This vegetable is also known as Indian round gourd or apple gourd.

GREEN PLANTAIN VEGETABLE
Kache Kele Ki Sabzi

INGREDIENTS

3 medium / 500 gm Green bananas (*kache kele*)
Lemon (*nimbu*) water (2½ cups / 500 ml water and add 2 tsp lemon juice)
3 tsp De-husked, split black gram (*dhuli urad dal*)
3 tsp De-husked, split Bengal gram (*chana dal*)
2 tsp Rice bran oil
Pinch, Asafoetida (*hing*)
¼ tsp Mustard (*sarson*) seeds
15 Curry leaves (*kadhipatta*)
1 dry Red chilli (*sookhi lal mirch*), broken into 2 pieces
2 tsp Coriander (*dhaniya*) powder
½ tsp Red chilli (*lal mirch*) powder
¼ tsp Mango powder (*amchur*)
Salt, to taste
2 Tbsp fresh Coriander (*dhaniya*) leaves, finely chopped

METHOD

- Peel and cut the green bananas into ¼-inch round discs and soak in the lemon water.

- Steam the green bananas in a double boiler / vegetable steamer for 12–15 minutes (see pgs. 218–19) until they are cooked through yet firm. Remove and set aside to cool.

- Mix both the lentils together. Wash well with 1 cup / 200 ml water, drain in a colander and set aside.

- Heat 2 tsp oil in a broad vessel for 30 seconds over medium heat. Add the asafoetida, mustard seeds and washed lentils. Sauté and cook until the lentils turn light brown in colour. Add curry leaves, dry broken chilli and the steamed banana pieces. Mix and lower the heat.

- Add coriander powder, chilli powder, mango powder, salt to taste and fresh coriander. Mix and cook over low heat for 3–4 minutes, stirring occasionally.

- Garnish with fresh coriander. Serve hot.

PER SERVING	1/3 CUP
Calories	110
Fat (grams)	2
Carbohydrates (grams)	21
Protein (grams)	2

- A great substitute for potatoes, green bananas are a much better source of both potassium and fibre.

- Soaking the cut banana pieces in lemon water helps to prevent darkening.

LEAFY MUSTARD GREENS
Sarso Ka Saag

INGREDIENTS

500 gm tender Mustard greens
(*sarson ke patte*)
2 tsp Mustard oil (*sarson ka tel*)
Pinch, Asafoetida (*hing*)
1/8 tsp Fenugreek seeds
(*methi dana*)
2 tsps Ginger (*adrak*), finely
chopped
1 tsp Green chillies (*hari mirch*),
finely chopped
2 dry Red chillies (*sookhi lal
mirch*), broken into 2 pieces
Salt, to taste

PER SERVING	1/3 CUP
Calories	30
Fat (grams)	2
Carbohydrates (grams)	1
Protein (grams)	2

METHOD

• Wash the mustard greens and drain in a colander. Pat dry with a kitchen towel.

• Remove the threads of the stems. Finely chop the stems and the remaining mustard greens. Set aside.

• In a heavy-bottom vessel over medium heat, heat the oil for 30 seconds. Add asafoetida, fenugreek seeds, ginger, green chillies and broken dry red chillies and mix. Add the chopped mustard greens and mix well. Cook covered for 2 minutes.

• Season to taste with salt and continue cooking until the water evaporates, stirring occasionally. Serve hot.

• Mustard greens are on the goitrogenic vegetable list. However, small amounts of this cooked, fibre-rich vegetable are fine for hypothyroidism.

• Though only available in winter in India, the same recipe can be made with amaranth leaves during the summer months.

SWEET POTATO & FENUGREEK LEAVES
Shakarkandi Aur Methi

INGREDIENTS

300 gm Sweet potato
(*shakarkandi*)
3 tsp (1 + 2) Rice bran oil
Pinch, Asafoetida (*hing*)
½ tsp Cumin (*jeera*) seeds
½ tsp Red chilli (*lal mirch*)
powder
2 tsp Coriander (*dhaniya*)
powder
¼ tsp Mango powder (*amchur*)
Salt, to taste
4 cups / 200 gm tightly packed
Fenugreek (*methi*) leaves,
washed, dried over kitchen
towel and finely chopped (see
pg. 216)

METHOD

- Pre-heat oven to 200°C.

- Wash and pat dry the sweet potatoes with a kitchen towel. Brush 1 tsp oil on their surface. Bake the potatoes for 20–30 minutes or until firm and cooked through. Cool at room temperature.

- Peel the sweet potatoes and cut into ¼-inch discs. Set aside.

- Heat 2 tsp oil in a broad pan for 30 seconds over medium heat. Add asafoetida, cumin seeds and sweet potato discs. Mix gently. Reduce the heat and add chilli powder, coriander powder, mango powder and salt to taste. Cook over medium heat for one minute, mixing frequently.

- Add the fenugreek leaves, cook for a minute over medium heat, mix and serve hot.

PER SERVING	½ CUP
Calories	142
Fat (grams)	2
Carbohydrates (grams)	27
Protein (grams)	4

- The combination of the iron-packed fenugreek leaves and potassium-filled sweet potato provides the long-lasting energy required by those who engage in strenuous activities, such as marathon runners.

- Baking times may differ depending upon the thickness of the sweet potato.

BOTTLE GOURD & GREEN GRAM LENTIL
Lauki Aur Moong Ki Dal

Serves: 6 (3 cups)
Suggested portion per serving: ½ cup

INGREDIENTS

¼ cup / 50 gm Skinned, split green gram (*dhuli moong dal*)
400 gm Bottle gourd (*lauki*)
½ tsp Rice bran oil
4 Cloves (*laung*)
⅛ tsp Cumin (*jeera*) seeds
2 cups / 400 ml Water
¼ tsp Turmeric (*haldi*) powder
Salt, to taste
2 Tbsp fresh Coriander (*dhaniya*) leaves, finely chopped

For the tempering:

1½ tsp Rice bran oil
2 tsp Ginger (*adrak*) julienne
Pinch, Asafoetida (*hing*)
¼ tsp Cumin (*jeera*) seeds
⅛ tsp freshly ground Black peppercorn (*sabut kali mirch*)

METHOD

- Wash and drain the split green gram in a colander just before cooking.

- Peel and cut bottle gourd into 1-inch cubes and immerse in water to avoid browning.

- Heat ½ tsp oil in a pressure cooker over medium heat for 30 seconds. Add the cloves, cumin seeds, lentil, bottle gourd pieces, 2 cups (400 ml) water, turmeric powder and salt to taste.

- Pressure cook over high heat to one whistle and simmer for 2 minutes. Turn off the heat, allow the pressure to release and remove the lid.

- Turn on the heat and bring the lentil to a boil over medium heat. Add the fresh coriander leaves, mix and transfer to a serving dish.

- **For the tempering**, heat 1½ tsp oil in a tempering ladle for 30 seconds. Add the ginger julienne and cook until the edges are light brown in colour, stirring frequently. Add the asafoetida, cumin seeds and black pepper. Immediately pour over the lentils and serve hot.

PER SERVING	½ CUP
Calories	92
Fat (grams)	4
Carbohydrates (grams)	11
Protein (grams)	3

- With subtle flavour and high water content, bottle gourd is easy to digest.

- Unlike most other lentils, there is no need to soak skinned, split green gram lentil before cooking, because it cooks fairly quickly.

BUTTER BEANS IN TOMATO GRAVY
Taridar Vaal Ki Sabzi

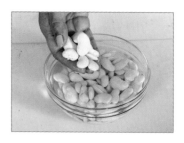   

INGREDIENTS

½ cup / 90 gm Butter beans
(*vaal*), washed, soaked in water
for 12 hours and drained
in colander
1¾ cups / 350 ml Water
⅛ tsp Salt
½ tsp (¼ + ¼) Turmeric (*haldi*)
powder
2 tsp Rice bran oil
¾ cup / 90 gm Onion (*pyaz*),
finely chopped (see pg. 215)
2 tsp Ginger (*adrak*), finely
chopped
¼ tsp Red chilli (*lal mirch*)
powder
3 medium-sized / 200 gm
Tomatoes (*tamatar*), liquidized
(see pg. 225)
Salt, to taste
1 Green chilli (*hari mirch*), slit
2 Tbsp fresh Coriander
(*dhaniya*) leaves, finely chopped
⅛ tsp Spice mix (*garam masala*)
powder (see pg. 222)

METHOD

- Pressure cook the soaked butter beans with water, ⅛ tsp salt and ¼ tsp turmeric powder to one whistle. Simmer for 15 minutes, turn off the heat and wait until the pressure releases. Remove the lid and set aside.

- In a broad pan over medium heat, heat the oil for 30 seconds. Add the onion and ginger. Fry until light golden brown, stirring occasionally. Add the remaining turmeric powder and chilli powder and mix.

- Add the liquidized tomatoes. Cook over medium heat, mixing frequently, until the mixture is reduced to half its volume.

- Add the pressure-cooked butter beans and salt to taste. Bring the mixture to a boil and simmer for 5 minutes. Add the green chilli, fresh coriander and spice mix powder. Serve hot.

PER SERVING	½ CUP
Calories	153
Fat (grams)	3
Carbohydrates (grams)	25.5
Protein (grams)	6

- Butter beans are a good source of protein and help build lean muscles – the fat-burning machinery of our body.

- The gravy of butter beans may thicken after some time; one can add hot water to get the desired consistency.

DRY COLOCASIA
Sookhi Arvi

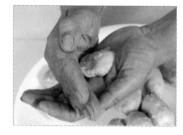

INGREDIENTS

300 gms Colocasia (*arvi*)
1½ cups / 300 ml Water
2 tsp Coriander (*dhaniya*) seeds
¼ tsp freshly ground Black peppercorn (*sabut kali mirch*)
3 tsp Mustard oil (*sarson ka tel*)
Pinch, Asafoetida (*hing*)
¼ tsp Carom (*ajwain*) seeds
¼ tsp Mango powder (*amchur*)
Salt, to taste
¼ tsp Green chillies (*hari mirch*), finely chopped
2 Tbsp fresh Coriander leaves, finely chopped

METHOD

• Place the colocasia in a small colander that fits into a pressure cooker. Set aside.

• Add 1½ cups / 300 ml of water to the pressure cooker. Place a cooking rack inside the pressure cooker. Place the colander with the colocasia on top of the cooking rack. Pressure cook over high heat to one whistle and simmer for 4 minutes. Turn off the heat and let the pressure release (see pg. 213). Remove the colocasia and set aside.

• Peel and press the colocasia using your palms. Set aside.

• Using a mortar and pestle, pound the coriander seeds into a coarse powder. Remove and set aside.

• In the same mortar and pestle, pound the black pepper into a coarse powder. Set aside.

• Heat the oil in a broad non-stick pan over medium heat for 30 seconds. Add asafoetida, carom seeds and colocasia. Toss gently.

• Reduce the heat and add coriander powder, black pepper powder, mango powder, salt and green chillies. Mix well. Cook for five minutes, turning occasionally or until light brown on both sides. Add the fresh coriander leaves. Mix and serve hot.

PER SERVING	3 PIECES
Calories	74
Fat (grams)	2
Carbohydrates (grams)	13
Protein (grams)	1

• Mustard oil is a good source of monounsaturated fatty acids and vitamin E, both of which have protective effects on the body.

• To ensure the quality of colocasia, select the ones that are firm and have rounded ends.

GARLIC-FLAVOURED SPINACH
Lehsuni Palak

INGREDIENTS

4 Black peppercorns (*sabut kali mirch*)
½ Black cardamom (*badi elaichi*), seeds only
2 Cloves (*laung*)
750 gm Spinach (*palak*)
2 tsp Rice bran oil
6 Cloves of garlic (*lasan*), peeled
2 tsp Ginger (*adrak*) paste (see pg. 212)
2 tsp Garlic paste (see pg. 212)
¼ tsp Red chilli (*lal mirch*) powder
Salt, to taste
½ tsp Jaggery (*gur*) powder

METHOD

- In a mortar and pestle, grind the black peppercorn, cloves and black cardamom seeds into a coarse powder.

- Cut and discard the hard stems of the spinach. Wash and drain in a colander. Chop the spinach leaves. Set aside.

- In a pan over medium heat, add the chopped spinach. Keep the pan covered for 2 minutes, stirring in-between. Remove from the pan and cool. Set aside.

- Coarsely grind the cooked spinach in a mixer along with any residual water. Set aside this spinach puree.

- In a broad pan over medium heat, heat the oil for 30 seconds. Add the garlic cloves, ginger paste and garlic paste. Mix and cook for 20 seconds. Add the red chilli powder and coarsely ground spice mixture; mix well.

- Add the pureed spinach, salt to taste and jaggery powder. Mix gently and bring the gravy to a boil. Simmer for 2–3 minutes. Serve hot.

PER SERVING	½ CUP
Calories	54
Fat (grams)	2
Carbohydrates (grams)	4
Protein (grams)	5

- It is important to retain any residual liquids while cooking vegetables as most of the nutritional value seeps into this liquid.

GRAVY BUTTON MUSHROOM
Rasedar Khumb

INGREDIENTS

250 gm medium-sized white Button mushrooms (*khumb*)
Lemon (*nimbu*) water (2½ cups / 500 ml water and ⅛ tsp lemon juice)
2 tsp Rice bran oil
3 medium / 150 gm Onions (*pyaz*), finely chopped (see pg. 215)
2 tsp Ginger (*adrak*), finely chopped
⅛ tsp Turmeric (*haldi*) powder
¼ tsp Red chilli (*lal mirch*) powder
3 medium / 200 gm Tomatoes (*tamatar*), liquidized (see pg. 225)
1½ Tbsp low-fat Yoghurt (*dahi*), whisked
1 tsp dry Fenugreek leaves (*kasoori methi*)
1 cup / 200 ml Water
Salt, to taste
⅛ tsp Spice mix (*garam masala*) (see pg. 222)

METHOD

- Wash the mushrooms in water and drain in a colander. Pat dry with a kitchen towel. Slit the stem and cut each mushroom into half or quarter to make into ¾-inch size. Dip them all in the lemon water. Remove and steam for 2 minutes. Set aside.

- Heat the oil in a heavy-bottom vessel over medium heat for 30 seconds. Add the chopped onion and ginger; cook over low heat until light brown, stirring occasionally. Add the turmeric and chilli powder. Mix well.

- Add the liquidized tomatoes. Mix and cook until the gravy thickens, stirring occasionally. Add the whisked yoghurt. Cook and stir continuously until it bubbles. Cook for another 2 minutes.

- Add the dry fenugreek leaves, steamed mushrooms, water and salt to taste. Bring the gravy to a boil over medium heat. Simmer for 5 minutes and add the spice mix powder. Serve hot.

PER SERVING	½ CUP
Calories	84
Fat (grams)	2
Carbohydrates (grams)	12.5
Protein (grams)	4

- Dipping mushrooms in lemon water helps them retain their whiteness.

- Mushrooms are a good source of potassium, making them ideal during hot summer months to keep you hydrated.

- *Kasoori methi* can be made at home by drying fresh fenugreek
  leaves. Once dry, crumble and store in an air-tight jar.

LENTIL STEW
Sambhar

INGREDIENTS

½ cup / 90 gm Yellow lentil (*arhar dal*), soaked in water for 30 minutes, drained
1½ cups / 110 gm Bottle gourd (*lauki*), cut into 1-inch pieces
½ cup / 60 gm Carrot (*gajar*), cut into ¼-inch round discs
½ cup / 65 gm Radish (*mooli*), cut into ¼-inch round discs
10 pieces / 90 gm Cauliflower (*phool gobi*), cut into ¾-inch florets
8 Haricot beans, cut into 1½-inch pieces
3½ cups / 700 ml Water
Salt, to taste

½ tsp Turmeric (*haldi*) powder
4 medium / 275 gm Tomatoes (*tamatar*), liquidized (see pg. 225)
2 tsp *Sambhar* powder (see pg. 223)
⅛ tsp Mango powder (*amchur*)
¼ tsp Jaggery (*gur*) powder
2 Tbsp fresh Coriander (*dhaniya*) leaves, finely chopped

For the tempering:
2 tsp Rice bran oil
Pinch, Asafoetida (*hing*)
½ tsp Mustard (*sarson*) seeds
12 Curry leaves (*kadhipatta*)
¼ tsp Red chilli (*lal mirch*) powder
1 tsp Coriander powder

METHOD

- In a pressure cooker, add the soaked yellow lentil with bottle gourd, carrot, radish, cauliflower, haricot beans, water, salt to taste and turmeric powder. Cook to one whistle. Turn off the heat. Wait until the pressure settles and remove the lid.

- Add the liquidized tomatoes to this lentil stew and bring the mixture to a boil. Lower the heat and simmer for 10 minutes.

- Add 2 tsp *sambhar* powder, mango powder, jaggery powder and fresh coriander leaves. Simmer for 2 more minutes.

- **For the tempering**, heat 2 tsp oil in a tempering ladle for 30 seconds. Add the asafoetida, mustard seeds, curry leaves, red chilli powder and coriander powder. Mix and immediately pour over the lentil stew. Serve hot.

PER SERVING	¾ CUP
Calories	62
Fat (grams)	2
Carbohydrates (grams)	11.5
Protein (grams)	1.5

- Lentil stew / *sambhar* is a popular dish from the southern region of India. Serve with Finger Millet Rice Cake / *Ragi Idli* (see pg. 90), Finger Millet Pancake / *Ragi Dosa* (see pg. 92) or Lacy Rice Pancake / *Rice Dosa* (see pg. 160) for a complete meal.

LONG GREEN BEANS WITH KIDNEY BEANS
Rajma Aur Lobia Ki Phali

INGREDIENTS

¼ cup / 50 gm Kidney beans
(*rajma*), soaked in water for
10 hours, drained
½ cup / 100 ml + 2 Tbsp Water
⅛ tsp Salt
¼ tsp Red chilli (*lal mirch*)
powder
1 tsp Coriander (*dhanyia*)
powder
250 gm Long green beans
(*lobia phali*)
3 tsp Rice bran oil
Pinch, Asafoetida (*hing*)
¼ tsp Cumin (*jeera*) seeds
⅛ tsp Turmeric (*haldi*) powder
Salt, to taste
1 Tbsp fresh Coriander leaves,
finely chopped

METHOD

. • Pressure cook the soaked kidney beans with ½ cup / 100 ml of water and ⅛ tsp salt over medium heat to one whistle. Simmer for 15 minutes and turn off the heat. Once the pressure settles, open the lid and transfer the beans along with the water to a large, broad pan. Cook until all the water evaporates, mixing occasionally. Add the chilli powder and coriander powder. Mix and set aside.

• Wash the long beans and pat dry with a kitchen towel. Remove their strings and cut the beans into 1-inch pieces. Set aside.

• Heat 2 tsp oil in a broad pan for 30 seconds over medium heat. Add the asafoetida, cumin seeds and turmeric powder. Add the long beans, salt to taste and 2 Tbsp water. Mix, cover and cook for 2 minutes, stirring occasionally.

• Uncover and cook open until all the residual water has evaporated. Reduce the heat. Add the cooked kidney beans and mix gently. Add the fresh coriander leaves, mix and serve hot.

PER SERVING	¾ CUP
Calories	116
Fat (grams)	4
Carbohydrates (grams)	15
Protein (grams)	5

• Kidney beans and long green beans both pack in a large amount of protein to help build muscle mass and heal the body from injuries.

• Long green beans are also known as *chawli* in Hindi.

MIX VEGETABLE CURRY
Sindhi Kadhi

INGREDIENTS

2 / 100 gm Drumstick (*sajjan ki phali*)
20 / 40 gm Cluster beans (*guar phali*)
7½ cups / 1.5 L (1½ + 6) Water
12 / 50 gm tender Okra (*bhindi*), washed, wiped, with head and tail removed
12 / 50 gm Haricot beans, washed, wiped, string removed and cut into 2-inch pieces
3 tsp Rice bran oil
Pinch, Asafoetida (*hing*)
¼ tsp Fenugreek seeds (*methi dana*)
¼ tsp Cumin (*jeera*) seeds
¼ tsp Mustard (*sarson*) seeds
15 Curry leaves (*kadhipatta*)
½ cup / 60 gm Gram flour (*besan*)
⅛ tsp Turmeric (*haldi*) powder
⅓ tsp Red chilli (*lal mirch*) powder
Salt, to taste
5 medium / 350 gm Tomatoes (*tamatar*), liquidized (see pg. 225)
2 tsp Ginger (*adrak*), finely chopped
¼ tsp Green chillies (*hari mirch*), finely chopped
⅛ tsp Mango powder (*amchur*)
2 Tbsp fresh Coriander (*dhaniya*) leaves, finely chopped

METHOD

- Cut the drumsticks into 2-inch pieces and string each piece of drumstick from all sides (see pg. 214). String the cluster beans and cut them into 2-inch pieces. Set aside.

- In a pan over medium heat, add 1½ cups of water, drumsticks and cluster beans. Cover and bring to a boil. Uncover and continue cooking over low heat until the pieces are firm and cooked through. Set aside.

- Steam the okra for two minutes and haricot beans for three minutes in a double boiler / vegetable steamer (see pgs. 218–19). Set aside.

- In a heavy-bottom vessel over medium heat, heat the oil for 30 seconds. Reduce the heat and add asafoetida, fenugreek seeds, cumin seeds, mustard seeds, curry leaves and gram flour. Roast, stirring frequently, until the flour turns light golden brown.

- Gradually add the remaining water and bring the gravy to a boil over medium heat, stirring constantly to avoid any lumps. Add the turmeric powder, chilli powder and salt to taste. Simmer for 20 minutes.

- Add the liquidized tomatoes, ginger and green chillies, and mix. Add mango powder, bring the gravy to a boil and simmer for 10 minutes. Add the cooked drumsticks and cluster beans. Mix and cook for another 2 minutes. Add the steamed okra, haricot beans and fresh coriander leaves; mix. Serve hot.

PER SERVING	¾ CUP
Calories	60
Fat (grams)	2
Carbohydrates (grams)	8.5
Protein (grams)	2

- Steaming vegetables and boiling them for a very short time allow them to keep their original colour and nutritional value intact.

- Drumsticks are a good source of B vitamins, which give this vegetable digestive properties.

STUFFED POINTED GOURD
Bharwa Parwal

INGREDIENTS

8–10 medium / 250 gm Pointed gourd (*parwal*)
125 gm low-fat Cottage cheese (*paneer*) (see pg. 206)
2 tsp Ginger (*adrak*), finely chopped
½ tsp Green chillies (*hari mirch*), finely chopped
2 tsp fresh Coriander (*dhaniya*) leaves, finely chopped
⅛ tsp Spice mix (*garam masala*) (see pg. 222)
Salt, to taste
2 tsp Rice bran oil
Pinch, Asafoetida (*hing*)
¼ tsp Cumin (*jeera*) seeds
Fresh coriander leaves, to garnish

METHOD

• Trim both the ends of the pointed gourds, scrape them with a blunt side of a knife and slit vertically three quarters of the way down, keeping the vegetable intact.

• Steam the pointed gourds in a double boiler / vegetable steamer for 6 minutes (see pgs. 218–19). Remove and set aside to cool. Remove the pulp and seeds from inside. Discard the hard seeds and reserve the pulp and soft seeds for later use.

• Grate the cottage cheese. Mix in with the reserved pulp and soft seeds, chopped ginger, green chillies, coriander leaves, spice mix and salt to taste. Set aside.

• Evenly stuff this cottage cheese mixture into the steamed pointed gourds and set aside.

• In a broad non-stick pan over medium heat, heat the oil for 30 seconds. Add the asafoetida, cumin seeds and stuffed pointed gourds. Fry, tossing frequently, until the skin of the vegetable starts turning light brown. Toss for a further 30 seconds and remove. Garnish with fresh coriander leaves. Serve hot.

PER SERVING	2½ PIECES
Calories	123
Fat (grams)	5
Carbohydrates (grams)	10
Protein (grams)	9

• The high fibre content of pointed gourd helps those suffering from digestive issues such as constipation.

• The high protein content of cottage cheese helps to keep one full for a longer time, making it an ideal food for weight management.

• Select pointed gourds that are firm and have bright green skins.

YELLOW PUMPKIN WITH GREEN PEAS
Kaddu Aur Hari Matar

INGREDIENTS

1¼ cup / 190 gm Green peas
(*hara matar*), shelled
500 gm Yellow pumpkin (*kaddu*)
Pinch, salt
Pinch, Asafoetida (*hing*)
¼ tsp Cumin (*jeera*) seeds
2 tsp Ginger (*adrak*), finely
chopped
1/8 tsp Turmeric (*haldi*) powder
1 Green chilli (*hari mirch*), slit
into 2 pieces
¼ tsp Red chilli (*lal mirch*)
powder
3 medium / 200 gm Tomatoes
(*tamatar*), liquidized (see
pg. 225)
2 Tbsp fresh Coriander
(*dhaniya*) leaves, finely chopped
Salt, to taste
4 tsp (1 + 1 + 2) Rice bran oil

METHOD

- Steam the peas for 2–3 minutes in a double boiler / vegetable steamer (see pgs. 218–19). Set aside.

- Peel and cut pumpkin into pieces of 1¼-inch width. Set aside.

- Heat a griddle (*tawa*) for 30 seconds over medium heat and brush with ½ tsp of oil. Arrange half of the pumpkin pieces and brush the top surface using ½ tsp of oil. Sprinkle a pinch of salt over the pumpkin pieces, cover and cook over low heat for 10 minutes on each side or until they are cooked through. Remove and set aside. Repeat the process for the remaining pumpkin pieces using the same amount of oil.

- In a heavy-bottom vessel over medium heat, heat the remaining oil for 30 seconds. Add the asafoetida, cumin seeds, ginger, turmeric powder and chilli powder. Add the liquidized tomatoes and, stirring occasionally, cook until the gravy is semi-thick. Add the grilled pumpkin pieces and mix gently. Add the steamed peas, salt to taste, slit green chilli and fresh coriander. Mix well. Cook for a minute, stirring occasionally, and serve hot.

PER SERVING	1/3 CUP
Calories	56
Fat (grams)	2
Carbohydrates (grams)	8.5
Protein (grams)	1.5

- Pumpkin is a high glycemic index vegetable, which, when consumed, can lead to a rise in sugar levels for diabetics. Portion sizes should be controlled.

- Pumpkins are available from light to dark yellow in colour; for better taste, use yellow pumpkins.

BOTTLE GOURD DUMPLINGS IN YOGHURT GRAVY
Lauki Kofta Kadhi

INGREDIENTS

250 gm Bottle gourd (*lauki*), peeled and grated

4 Tbsp / 40 gm levelled Gram flour (*besan*)

½ tsp Ginger (*adrak*) paste (see pg. 212)

1 Tbsp fresh Coriander (*dhaniya*) leaves, finely chopped

⅛ tsp Salt

1 tsp Rice bran oil for roasting

For the gravy:

2 cups / 400 gm Sour yoghurt (*dahi*)

2 Tbsp / 20 gm levelled Gram flour

2 tsp Ginger paste (see pg. 212)

⅛ tsp Green chilli (*hari mirch*) paste (see pg. 212)

¼ tsp Turmeric (*haldi*) powder

Salt, to taste

2 cups / 400 ml Water

2 Tbsp fresh Coriander leaves, finely chopped

For the tempering:

2 tsp Rice bran oil

Pinch, Asafoetida (*hing*)

½ tsp Cumin (*jeera*) seeds

¼ tsp Red chilli (*lal mirch*) powder

2 dry Red chillies (*sookhi lal mirch*), broken into 2 pieces

METHOD

- Mix the grated bottle gourd with the gram flour, ginger paste, chopped coriander and salt. Divide the mixture into 15 equal portions and shape into round dumplings.

- Heat the pancake puff pan for a minute. Brush the moulds with ½ tsp oil. Place the dumplings into each mould and cover with a lid. Cook over medium-high heat until the edges begin to brown. Flip each one and cook for a minute or until it is light golden brown. Remove and repeat the process with the remaining dumplings using ½ tsp oil. Set aside.

- In a pan, whisk the yoghurt with gram flour, ginger paste, chilli paste and turmeric powder. Season to taste with salt. Whisk to a smooth paste. Add water and whisk well again.

- Transfer into a deep pan, bringing the gravy to a boil over medium heat, stirring frequently.

- Add the dumplings to the gravy. Bring to a boil, simmer for 5 minutes, add fresh coriander and turn off the heat.

- **For the tempering**, heat 2 tsp rice bran oil in a tempering ladle for 20 seconds over medium heat.

- Add the asafoetida, cumin seeds, chilli powder and broken chillies. Immediately pour over the gravy and serve hot.

PER SERVING	¾ CUP
Calories	92
Fat (grams)	4
Carbohydrates (grams)	11
Protein (grams)	8

- Traditionally, dumplings (*kofta*) are deep fried. Cooking the dumplings in a pancake puff pan allows the nutritional value of the vegetable to stay intact while keeping the calories low.

- Yoghurt is a good source of protein with almost 8 grams per cup.

WATER CHESTNUT AND MUSHROOM
Singhara Aur Khumb

INGREDIENTS
125 gm Button mushroom (*khumb*)
Lemon (*nimbu*) water
(2½ cups / 500 ml water and
⅛ tsp lemon juice)

For the Tomato Masala:
⅛ tsp Rice bran oil
⅛ tsp Red chilli (*lal mirch*)
powder
100 gm / 1 large Tomato
(*tamatar*), grated (see pg. 224)
Salt, to taste

2 tsp Rice bran oil
Pinch, Asafoetida (*hing*)
¼ tsp Cumin (*jeera*) seeds
2 tsp Ginger (*adrak*), finely
chopped
½ tsp Green chilli (*hari mirch*),
finely chopped
12 Water chestnuts (*singhara*),
peeled and vertically cut into
2 pieces

Salt, to taste
1 cup / 50 gm Spring onion
leaves (*hara pyaz ki patte*), finely
chopped (see pg. 216)
Pinch, Black peppercorn
(*sabut kali mirch*) powder

METHOD
• Wash the mushrooms, drain
in a colander and pat dry with
a kitchen towel. Discard the
stem and cut each mushroom
into half or quarter, to make
into ¾-inch size. Dip into the
lemon water, remove and
steam in a double boiler /
vegetable steamer for
1 minute. Set aside.

• Heat the oil in a pan over
medium heat for 10 seconds.
Add the red chilli powder
and grated tomato. Season

to taste with salt. Cook over
low heat until the mixture
thickens and set aside.

• Heat the oil in a broad pan
over medium heat for 30
seconds. Add the asafoetida,
cumin seeds, chopped ginger,
green chilli, water chestnut
and salt to taste. Cover and
cook for 2 minutes. Uncover
and cook for a minute. Add
the steamed mushrooms and
tomato masala, and continue
cooking over medium heat
for a minute. Add the finely
chopped spring onion leaves
and black peppercorn. Mix
gently and serve hot.

PER SERVING	½ CUP
Calories	82
Fat (grams)	2
Carbohydrates (grams)	12
Protein (grams)	4

• Mushroom and water chestnut are both good sources of potassium, which helps in reducing water retention, a common consequence of hypothyroidism.

• Water chestnut is a seasonal vegetable generally available in India in the autumn season.

WHOLE RED LENTIL WITH GOOSEFOOT LEAVES
Bathua Aur Kale Masoor Ki Dal

Serves: 4 (2 cups)
Suggested portion per serving: ½ cup

INGREDIENTS

4 cups / 200 gm tightly packed Goosefoot leaves (*bathua*), washed, dried over kitchen towel and finely chopped
½ cup / 90 gm Whole red lentil (*kale masoor*), washed, soaked in plenty of water for 30 minutes and drained in a colander
1¾ cups / 350 ml Water
Salt to taste
¼ tsp Turmeric (*haldi*) powder
2 tsp Ginger (*adrak*), finely chopped
¼ tsp Spice mix (*garam masala*) (see pg. 222)
¼ tsp Mango powder (*amchur*)

For the tempering:
2 tsp Rice bran oil
Pinch, Asafoetida (*hing*)
½ tsp Cumin (*jeera*) seeds
¼ tsp Red chilli (*lal mirch*) powder

METHOD

• Steam chopped goosefoot leaves in a vegetable steamer for 1½ minutes (see pg. 218). Remove and set aside to cool.

• Pressure cook the soaked whole red lentil – with the water, salt to taste and turmeric powder – to one whistle. Simmer for 10 minutes and turn off the heat. Wait until the pressure settles and remove the lid. Add ginger, spice mix, mango powder and steamed goosefoot leaves, and mix. Bring to a boil over moderate heat and simmer for two minutes.

• Transfer to a serving dish and season with tempering.

• **For tempering**, heat 2 tsp oil in a tempering ladle for 10 seconds. Add the asafoetida, cumin seeds and red chilli powder. Pour over the lentils immediately. Serve hot.

PER SERVING	½ CUP
Calories	192
Fat (grams)	6
Carbohydrates (grams)	33
Protein (grams)	12

• Goosefoot leaves are an excellent source of vitamins A and C, making it ideal post-workout fuel to repair the body.

• Whole red lentils are a good source of folic acid and iron, both nutrients required in higher amounts during pregnancy.

RICE & BREADS

BARNYARD MILLET WITH BOTTLE GOURD
Samak Ke Chawal

INGREDIENTS

¼ cup / 50 gm Barnyard millet
(*samak ke chawal*)
4 cups / 800 ml Water
3 tsp (1 + 2) Rice bran oil
300 gm tender Bottle
gourd (*lauki*)
¼ tsp Cumin (*jeera*) seeds
Pinch, salt
2 tsp Ginger (*adrak*), finely
chopped
¼ tsp Green chilli (*hari mirch*),
finely chopped
3 Tbsp Peanuts (*moongphalli*),
roasted, skinned (see pg. 211)
2 Tbsp fresh Coriander
(*dhaniya*) leaves, finely chopped

METHOD

- Wash and soak barnyard millet in water for 15 minutes, drain using a colander and set aside. Place 4 cups / 800 ml water in a pan and bring to boil over medium heat. Add soaked barnyard millet and cook for 1 minute. Immediately drain in a micro sieve, add 1 tsp oil and keep mixing gently until the millet cools to room temperature (see pg. 221).

- Peel and cut thin slices of bottle gourd. Cut each slice into thin small strips. Join all the strips together and further cut into small pieces. Set aside.

- Heat 2 tsp oil in a heavy-bottom vessel for 30 seconds over medium heat. Add cumin seeds, bottle gourd pieces and a pinch of salt. Mix well, cover and cook for 30 seconds. Remove the lid and cook until water evaporates, stirring occasionally.

- Lower the heat. Add the cooked barnyard millet, salt to taste, ginger, green chilli, peanuts and chopped coriander. Over medium heat, mix gently for a minute and serve hot.

PER SERVING	²/₃ CUP
Calories	274
Fat (grams)	13
Carbohydrates (grams)	26
Protein (grams)	8

- Unlike other millets, barnyard millet is very easy to digest and contains more protein, fibre and iron than other whole grains.

- Follow the proper cooking time of barnyard millet, as it has a tendency to become lumpy.

RICE LENTIL HOTCHPOTCH
Sabjiyon Ki Khichdi

Serves: 4 (4 cups)
Suggested portion per serving: 1 cup

INGREDIENTS

½ cup / 90 gm Brown rice
½ cup / 100 gm Skinned, split green gram (*dhuli moong dal*)
½ cup / 40 gm Haricot beans, cut into thin slant pieces (see pg. 214)
¼ cup / 40 gm Peas (*hara mattar*)
3 cups / 600 ml Water
Salt, to taste
¼ tsp Turmeric (*haldi*) powder
2 tsp Ginger (*adrak*), finely chopped
2 medium / 140 gm Tomatoes (*tamatar*), grated (see pg. 224)
2 Tbsp fresh Coriander (*dhaniya*) leaves, finely chopped

For the tempering:

2 tsp Rice bran oil
Pinch, Asafoetida (*hing*)
2 tsp Ginger (*adrak*), slivered
½ tsp Cumin (*jeera*) seeds
½ tsp Red chilli (*lal mirch*) powder

METHOD

• Wash and soak rice in water for 30 minutes, drain in a colander and set aside. Wash split green lentil in water just before cooking. Drain and set aside.

• Steam beans and peas in a double boiler / vegetable steamer for 2 minutes (see pgs. 218–19). Set aside.

• In a pressure cooker, add the soaked rice and green lentil with 3 cups (600 ml) of water, salt, turmeric powder and chopped ginger. After one whistle, turn off the heat. Once the pressure settles, open the lid, add the grated tomato and bring the mixture to a boil. Add cooked beans, peas and chopped coriander. Mix well and transfer to a serving bowl.

• For the tempering, heat 2 tsp oil in a tempering ladle for 20 seconds over medium heat. Add asafoetida and slivered ginger. Cook for 10 seconds. Add cumin seeds and ¼ tsp chilli powder; mix. Pour over the rice lentil hotpotch / *khichdi*. Serve hot.

PER SERVING	1 CUP
Calories	185
Fat (grams)	5
Carbohydrates (grams)	30
Protein (grams)	5

• This is an all-in-one dish that provides carbohydrates, proteins and goodness of vegetables – a great comfort food.

RED RICE PILAF
Kerala Pulao

INGREDIENTS

½ cup / 90 gm Red rice
1¼ / 250 ml Water
2 tsp (¼ + ¼ + 1½) Rice bran oil
1 cup / 135 gm Red pumpkin (kaddoo), cut into 1-inch cubes
1 cup / 75 gm Eggplant (baingan), cut into 1-inch cubes
2 tsp De-husked, split black gram (dhuli urad dal)
2 tsp De-husked, split Bengal gram (chana dal)
¼ tsp Mustard (sarson) seeds
20 Curry leaves (kadhipatta)
¼ tsp Red chilli (lal mirch) powder
⅛ tsp Turmeric (haldi) powder
3 medium / 200 gm Tomatoes (tamatar), liquidized (see pg. 225)
2 tsp Ginger (adrak), finely chopped
1 Green chilli, slit lengthwise into half
Salt, to taste
2 Tbsp (1 + 1) fresh Coriander (dhaniya) leaves, finely chopped
2 Tbsp (1 + 1) fresh Coconut (nariyal), grated (see pg. 210)

METHOD

- Wash and soak the red rice in water for 1 hour. Drain using a colander. Set aside.

- Boil 1¼ cup (250 ml) of water in a broad pan. Add the drained rice and bring to a boil. Cover the pan and simmer over low heat for 20–30 minutes or until all the water evaporates and the rice is soft. Set aside.

- Heat a griddle (tawa) over medium heat for 30 seconds and brush with ⅛ tsp of oil. Arrange the pumpkin pieces and brush the top of the pieces with ⅛ tsp of oil. Cover and cook over low heat for 10 minutes on each side. Remove from heat and set aside.

- Repeat the same process with the eggplant using ¼ tsp oil (⅛ + ⅛) and set aside.

- In a bowl, mix the split black gram and the split Bengal gram together. Wash well, drain and set aside.

- Heat 1½ tsp oil in a broad pan over medium heat for 30 seconds. Add the washed lentils, stir and cook until light brown. Add the mustard seeds, curry leaves, chilli powder and turmeric powder. Mix well. Add liquidized tomatoes and cook for 2 minutes. Add cooked red rice and mix.

- Add the cooked pumpkin and eggplant pieces, ginger, slit green chilli, salt, 1 Tbsp chopped coriander and 1 Tbsp grated coconut to the red rice mix. Stir gently. Garnish with the remaining chopped coriander and coconut. Serve hot.

PER SERVING	¾ CUP
Calories	177
Fat (grams)	5
Carbohydrates (grams)	28
Protein (grams)	5

- Red rice has high amounts of fibre, which helps keep the stomach full for longer, prevents blood sugar levels from spiking and aids in digestion.

- After simmering, the rice will take 25–30 minutes to cook.

ZUCCHINI & BROCCOLI PILAF
Zucchini Aur Broccoli Ka Pulao

INGREDIENTS

5 cups / 1 L Water
½ cup / 90 gm Brown rice, washed, soaked in water for 30 minutes, drained in a colander
2 tsp Rice bran oil
2 Tbsp Onion (*pyaz*), finely chopped
2 cups / 200 gm Zucchini, cut into 1-inch slant pieces (see pg. 215)
2 cups / 160 gm Broccoli, cut into ¾-inch florets (see pg. 214)
Salt, to taste
¼ tsp freshly ground Black peppercorn (*sabut kali mirch*)
2 Tbsp Spring onion leaves (*hara pyaz ke patte*), finely chopped

METHOD

• Place 5 cups (1 L) water in a pan to boil over medium heat. Add the soaked rice and bring to a boil. Cook covered over low heat until the rice is soft and grains are intact. Drain into a colander. Set aside.

• Heat 2 tsp oil in a broad pan for 30 seconds over medium heat, add onion and cook for 10 seconds. Add zucchini pieces and broccoli florets. Cook for a minute, stirring occasionally.

• Add the cooked rice, salt to taste, black pepper powder and chopped spring onion. Stir gently for a minute and serve hot.

PER SERVING	¾ CUP
Calories	203
Fat (grams)	5
Carbohydrates (grams)	25
Protein (grams)	3

• Though there is a very small difference in calories between white rice and brown rice, the higher-caloric brown rice is far superior nutritionally as it contains fibre, protein and the potent antioxidant, selenium.

• Zucchini is also known as courgette. It has a mild flavour and is eaten with its skin.

RIDGED GOURD RICE
Turai Ke Chawal

INGREDIENTS
¼ cup / 45 gm Brown rice
5 cups / 1 L Water
500 gm Ridged gourd (*turai*)
2 tsp Rice bran oil
Pinch, Asafoetida (*hing*)
¼ tsp Cumin (*jeera*) seeds
Pinch, salt
2 tsp Ginger (*adrak*), finely chopped
2 tsp soft Coriander stem (*mulayam danthal*), finely chopped
2 Tbsp Peanuts (*moongphalli*) roasted, skinned (see pg. 211), to garnish

METHOD
• Wash and soak brown rice in water for 30 minutes. Drain and set aside.

• Place 5 cups (1 L) water in a pan over medium heat. Add the soaked rice and bring to a boil. Cover and cook over low heat until the rice is soft. Drain and set aside.

• Peel the ridged gourd and cut into ¼-inch round slices. Set aside.

• Heat 2 tsp oil in a broad pan for 30 seconds over medium heat. Add the asafoetida, cumin seeds, ridged gourd pieces and a pinch of salt. Cover and cook for a minute, stirring occasionally. Remove the lid and stir gently until the water evaporates and the gourd pieces are cooked through but firm.

• Add the cooked rice and gently mix well. Add ginger, coriander stem and salt. Cook for a minute, mixing gently. Garnish with peanuts and serve hot.

PER SERVING	¾ CUP
Calories	94.5
Fat (grams)	2.5
Carbohydrates (grams)	16
Protein (grams)	3

• Ridged gourd contains properties that help reduce acidity, improve digestion and keep blood sugar levels within normal limits.

SORGHUM & LENTIL FUSION
Jowar Khichdi

INGREDIENTS

½ cup / 100 gm Sorghum
(jowar)
¼ cup / 50 gm Whole green
gram (sabut moong dal)
2½ cups / 500 ml Water
¼ tsp Turmeric (haldi) powder
Salt, to taste

For the tempering:

2 tsp Rice bran oil
Pinch, Asafoetida (hing)
2 tsp Ginger (adrak), slivered
¼ tsp Cumin (jeera) seeds
1 Green chilli (hari mirch), slit
lengthwise into half
1 Tbsp fresh Coriander
(dhaniya) leaves, finely chopped
¼ tsp Red chilli (lal mirch)
powder

METHOD

• Wash and soak sorghum in water for 15 hours. Drain and set aside.

• Wash and soak whole green gram in water for 45 minutes. Drain and set aside.

• In a pressure cooker, add the soaked sorghum with 2½ cup / 500 ml water. After one whistle, simmer for 30 minutes and turn off the heat. Once the pressure settles, open the lid.

• Add the soaked green gram, turmeric and salt. Close the lid and pressure cook for one whistle. Simmer for 15 minutes, turn off the heat and allow the pressure to settle.

• Open the lid and check the sorghum lentil fusion / jowar khichdi. It should be of semi-thick consistency. If it's too thick, add ¼–½ cup (50–100 ml) hot water. Over medium heat, cook the mixture to desired consistency. Transfer to a serving bowl and serve with the tempering.

• **For the tempering**, heat 2 tsp oil in a tempering ladle for 20 seconds over medium heat. Add the asafoetida and slivered ginger and cook for 10 seconds. Add cumin seeds, slit green chilli, chopped coriander and ¼ tsp chilli powder mix. Pour over the sorghum lentil fusion / jowar khichdi. Serve hot.

PER SERVING	1/3 CUP
Calories	245
Fat (grams)	3
Carbohydrates (grams)	33
Protein (grams)	8

• The high protein and iron content of sorghum, along with protein-filled whole green gram, makes this dish perfect for building strength and energy.

• Sorghum takes long to cook, but don't shorten the process as uncooked sorghum is difficult to digest.

• Shown served with Spinach Yoghurt (see pg. 185).

SPICY LENTIL RICE
Bisi Bele Bhaath

INGREDIENTS

For the Spicy Lentil Masala:
½ tsp De-husked, split Bengal gram (chana dal)
½ tsp De-husked, split black gram (dhuli urad dal)
⅛ tsp Fenugreek seeds (methi dana)
1 dry Red chilli (sookhi lal mirch)
2 tsp Coriander (dhaniya) seeds
¾ tsp Cumin (jeera) seeds
½ tsp Poppy (khus khus) seeds

Other ingredients:
⅓ cup / 55 gm Red double beans (badi lal sem ke beej)
¼ cup / 45 gm Small grain rice (chote chawal)
¼ cup / 50 gm Yellow lentil (arhar dal)
⅓ cup / 50 gm Haricot beans, washed, wiped, string removed and cut into 1-inch pieces
⅓ cup / 50 gm Carrot (gajar), peeled and cut into ¼-inch semi-circle pieces
6 / 50 gm Baby onions (choti pyaz), peeled
2 cups / 400 ml Water
⅛ tsp Turmeric (haldi) powder
2 large / 150 gm Tomatoes (tamatar), liquidized (see pg. 225)
2 Tbsp fresh Coriander leaves, finely chopped
Salt, to taste

For the tempering:
2 tsp Rice bran oil
Pinch, Asafoetida (hing)
¼ tsp Mustard (sarson) seeds
¼ tsp Red chilli (lal mirch) powder
20 Curry leaves (kadhipatta)

METHOD

- Wash and soak the red double beans in water for 12 hours. Drain and set aside.

- Wash and soak the rice and yellow lentil in water for 30 minutes. Drain and set aside.

- Heat a pan over medium heat for 10 seconds and place all the ingredients for the masala. Dry roast over low heat, stirring occasionally until light golden brown. Remove and cool at room temperature. Grind in a mixer and set aside.

- Steam haricot beans in a double boiler / vegetable steamer for three minutes (see pgs. 218–19). Set aside.

- In a pressure cooker, add the soaked lentils, rice, red double beans, carrot and baby onions with 2 cups / 400 ml water, turmeric powder and salt. After one whistle, simmer for four minutes and turn off the heat. Once the pressure settles, open the lid, add liquidized tomatoes and cook for one minute over medium heat. Add the masala, steamed haricot beans and chopped coriander. Mix well.

- **For the tempering,** heat 2 tsp oil in a tempering ladle for 20 seconds over medium heat. Add the asafoetida, mustard seeds, chilli powder and curry leaves and pour over the rice. Serve hot.

PER SERVING	1 ½ CUP
Calories	245
Fat (grams)	3
Carbohydrates (grams)	33
Protein (grams)	8

- This is a complete meal with carbohydrates derived from the rice, protein from the lentils and lots of vitamins, minerals and fibre from the vegetables.

- Spicy lentil rice may thicken after some time; you can add hot water to bring it to the desired consistency.
- Shown served with Mixed Vegetable Yoghurt (see pg. 174).

SPICY VEGETABLE PILAF
Subz Biryani

INGREDIENTS

For the Yoghurt Mixture:
¼-inch Cinnamon (*dalchini*) stick
4 Cloves (*laung*)
8 whole Black peppercorns (*sabut kali mirch*)
1 Black cardamom (*badi elaichi*) seeds
20 Mint (*pudina*) leaves
3 Tbsp low-fat Yoghurt (*dahi*), whisked
¼ tsp Red chilli (*lal mirch*) powder
⅛ tsp Turmeric (*haldi*) powder

For the Pilaf:
2 tsp Rice bran oil
2 Bay leaves (*tej patta*)
1 / 70 gm Onion (*pyaz*), cut into long slices
1 tsp Garlic (*lasan*) paste (see pg. 212)
½ tsp Green chilli (*hari mirch*) paste (see pg. 212)
12 / 100 gm Baby onions (*choti pyaz*), peeled
1 medium / 85 gm Carrot (*gajar*), cut into 1-inch slant pieces
12 / 85 gm Haricot beans, cut into 1-inch slant pieces
½ cup / 100 gm Cauliflower (*phool gobi*), cut into ½-inch florets
Pinch, salt
½ cup / 90 gm Brown rice, cooked (see pg. 220)
½ cup / 80 gm Green peas (*hara mattar*), steamed for 3 minutes (see pgs. 218–19)
2 tsp fresh Coriander (*dhaniya*) leaves, finely chopped

METHOD

- **For the yoghurt mixture,** use a mortar and pestle to grind cinnamon, cloves, black peppercorns and black cardamom seeds to a coarse powder. Set aside this powder mixture.

- Use a mortar and pestle to grind 20 mint leaves to a coarse paste. Set aside.

- Mix whisked yoghurt with coarse powder mixture, red chilli, turmeric powder and mint paste. Set aside.

- **For the pilaf,** heat 2 tsp oil in a broad vessel for 30 seconds over medium heat. Add bay leaves, onion, garlic and chilli paste. Cook for 30 seconds, stirring continuously. Add baby onion and sauté for another 30 seconds.

- Add carrots, beans, cauliflower and a pinch of salt. Cover and cook over medium heat for 2 minutes, stirring occasionally. Uncover. Add the cooked rice, salt and the yoghurt mixture. Mix well but gently.

- Add the steamed peas and chopped coriander leaves. Mix well and serve hot.

PER SERVING	1 CUP
Calories	140
Fat (grams)	4
Carbohydrates (grams)	18
Protein (grams)	8

- A wide variety of vegetables, along with brown rice, makes this recipe fibre-packed and keeps you satisfied and full.

BLACK GRAM FLOUR BREAD
Kale Chane Ki Roti

INGREDIENTS

9 Tbsp slightly heaped / 90 gm
Black gram flour (*kale chane
ka atta*)
¼ tsp Salt
¼ tsp Fruit salt
1 Tbsp low-fat Yoghurt (*dahi*)
Water to make the dough
1 Tbsp / 10 gm Black gram flour
for dusting
1½ tsp Clarified butter (*ghee*)

METHOD

• Sieve the gram flour with the salt and fruit salt. Add yoghurt and mix well. Knead into a semi-hard dough with sufficient water. Cover with a damp cloth and let it stand for 10 minutes.

• Divide the dough into 6 equal portions and shape them into flat balls. Dust each ball with gram flour and gently roll into 3½-inch discs with a rolling pin, dusting in-between.

• Place a disc on a moderately hot griddle (*tawa*) and cook for 30 seconds. Flip and cook until light brown spots appear on the bottom side.

• Remove with tongs and roast over an open flame until light golden brown on both sides.

• Smear ¼ tsp clarified butter on top and serve immediately.

• Repeat the same process to prepare the remaining discs.

PER SERVING	2 PIECES
Calories	185
Fat (grams)	4.5
Carbohydrates (grams)	26
Protein (grams)	10

• With high amounts of protein and iron, black gram flour tends to be difficult to digest. The fruit salt and yoghurt help make it light and easy on the stomach.

• Black gram flour is a good source of the bone-building mineral, calcium.
• Shown served with Curried Black-eyed Peas (see pg. 112).

CRISPY RICE BREAD
Akki Roti

INGREDIENTS

6 levelled Tbsp / 60 gm Rice (*chawal*) flour
2½ tsp (½ + 2) Rice bran oil
¼ tsp Cumin (*jeera*) seeds
¾ cup / 90 gm Onion (*pyaz*), finely chopped (see pg. 215)
¼ tsp Green chilli (*hari mirch*), finely chopped
2 Tbsp fresh Coriander (*dhaniya*) leaves, finely chopped
Pinch, salt
Boiling water to prepare the dough
1 Tbsp / 10 gm Rice flour for dusting

METHOD

- Heat a broad pan over medium heat for 30 seconds. Add 6 Tbsp rice flour and roast, stirring constantly for 1 minute. Remove, cool at room temperature and set aside.

- Heat ½ tsp oil in a pan for 20 seconds over medium heat. Add the cumin seeds, onion, green chilli and coriander leaves. Cook for a minute, stirring constantly. Remove and set aside this mixture to cool.

- Mix the roasted rice flour, salt and onion mixture. Gradually add hot water to make the dough. Knead well to make a smooth dough that is neither too hard nor too soft.

- Divide the dough into 4 equal portions and shape them into round, flat balls.

- Dust each ball with rice flour and gently roll into 4-inch discs with a rolling pin, dusting in-between.

- Heat a griddle (*tawa*) over medium heat for 30 seconds and brush with oil. Carefully lift and place a disc on the griddle. After one minute, flip the rice bread using a flat spatula and continue cooking for another minute. Drizzle ½ tsp oil and cook until light golden brown on both sides. Serve immediately.

- Repeat the same process to prepare remaining discs.

PER SERVING	2 PIECES
Calories	122
Fat (grams)	4.5
Carbohydrates (grams)	21
Protein (grams)	2

- Opt for rice flour during the summer as it is lighter and easier to digest than wheat flour.

- Cook the Crispy Rice Bread soon after preparing the dough. Hot water helps to bind the dough well, or else the dough can form cracks while rolling out.

LACY RICE PANCAKE
Chawal Ka Dosa

INGREDIENTS

¼ cup / 40 gm Rice (*chawal*) flour

¼ cup / 30 gm Onion (*pyaz*), finely chopped (see pg. 215)

¼ tsp Green chilli (*hari mirch*), finely chopped

2 tsp Curry leaves (*kadhipatta*), finely chopped

⅛ tsp Cumin (*jeera*) seeds

¼ tsp Salt

½ cup (100 ml) Water

1 tsp Rice bran oil

METHOD

- In a bowl, mix rice flour, onion, green chilli, curry leaves, cumin seeds and salt with ½ cup of water. Prepare a batter of pouring consistency and set aside for 30 minutes.

- Heat a griddle (*tawa*) over medium heat for 40 seconds. Mix the batter well. Pour half the batter with a deep ladle in the center of the griddle creating a web. Drizzle ½ tsp oil on the edges of the pancake. Cook until the edges begin to brown, flip and cook for another 20 seconds. Flip again, fold and serve hot.

- Check the pouring consistency of the batter and, if required, add an additional ½ Tbsp water. Repeat the same process for the other pancake.

PER SERVING	2 PANCAKES
Calories	188
Fat (grams)	5.5
Carbohydrates (grams)	32
Protein (grams)	1

- Rice flour makes these pancakes a simple and light dish for any time of the day.

- If the batter is not of pouring consistency, it will not create a web. Make sure to measure the water while making the pancakes.

• Shown served with Bottle Gourd & Green Gram Lentil (see pg. 119).

MAIZE & SPRING ONION BREAD
Makka Aur Hara Pyaz Ka Paratha

INGREDIENTS

5 Tbsp levelled / 50 gm Maize flour (*makke ka atta*)

2 Tbsp levelled / 20 gm Gram flour (*besan*)

½ cup / 25 gm, Spring onion (*hara pyaz*), finely chopped (see pg. 216)

Pinch, Asafoetida (*hing*)

1/8 tsp Red chilli (*lal mirch*) powder

1/8 tsp Carom (*ajwain*) seeds

1/8 tsp Salt

Lukewarm water to prepare the dough

1 Tbsp (10 gm) Maize flour (*makke ka atta*) for dusting

2 tsp Mustard oil (*sarson ka tel*)

METHOD

- In a bowl, sieve the maize flour with the gram flour. Add the chopped spring onion leaves, asafoetida, chilli powder, carom seeds and salt. Knead into a dough (neither too hard nor too soft) with sufficient water.

- Divide the dough into 4 equal portions. Knead each portion gently and shape into flat balls. Dust each ball with maize flour and gently roll into 2-inch discs with a rolling pin.

- Apply a little oil, sprinkle maize flour on the disc and fold into a money bag. Flatten and dust lightly with maize flour.

- Now roll into 4-inch discs. Carefully lift and place a disc on a heated griddle (*tawa*). After a minute, flip the disc using a flat spatula and continue cooking for one minute.

- Drizzle the disc with 1/3 tsp oil and continue cooking until light golden brown on both sides. Serve hot.

- Repeat the same process to prepare the remaining discs.

PER SERVING	2 PIECES
Calories	133
Fat (grams)	4.5
Carbohydrates (grams)	21
Protein (grams)	2

- Maize flour is rich in phosphorus, magnesium, manganese, zinc, copper, iron and selenium – all of which are important trace minerals for immunity, energy and healing.

- Prepare the dough just before you plan to serve, or else it tends to become moist and difficult to roll.

MIXED MILLET BREAD
Mishrit Anaaj Ki Roti

INGREDIENTS

2 Tbsp levelled / 20 gm Pearl millet (*bajra*) flour
2 Tbsp levelled / 20 gm Sorghum (*jowar*) flour
2 Tbsp levelled / 20 gm Finger millet (*ragi*) flour
1 Tbsp levelled / 10 gm Soy (*soya*) flour
¼ tsp Salt
Hot water to make the dough
1 Tbsp levelled / 10 gm Pearl millet flour for dusting
2 tsp Clarified butter (*ghee*)

METHOD

- Sieve the pearl millet flour, sorghum flour, finger millet flour and soy flour with salt. Knead well with hot water. Keep kneading, adding a little water in-between, until the dough feels smooth and shows no cracks on the surface.

- Divide the dough into 4 equal portions. Take one portion, knead slightly and shape into a flat ball. Dust with pearl millet flour and gently flatten using your palm and fingers. Dust the rolling board, place the flattened disc on the board, sprinkle a little pearl millet flour on top and gently roll out into a 4-inch disc.

- Place a griddle (*tawa*) over medium heat. Carefully lift and place the disc on the griddle. After one minute, flip the disc using a flat spatula and cook for one minute.

- Remove with tongs and roast over an open flame until light golden brown on both sides.

- Smear ½ tsp clarified butter on top and serve immediately.

- Repeat the same process to prepare the remaining discs.

PER SERVING	2 PIECES
Calories	174
Fat (grams)	3.5
Carbohydrates (grams)	31
Protein (grams)	4.5

- Kneading each disc dough is important, or else the bread will crack due to the lack of gluten in the millet flour.

- Mixed millet bread is ideally eaten during the winter as the heat-inducing property of the protein-rich millets helps warm the body.

• Shown served with Gravy-Style Indian Baby Pumpkin (see pg. 115).

RICE BREAD
Chawal Ki Roti

   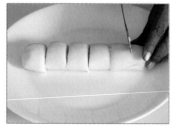

INGREDIENTS

7 Tbsp levelled / 70 gm Rice (*chawal*) flour
½ cup / 100 ml Water
1 tsp Rice bran oil
⅛ tsp Salt
1 Tbsp / 10 gm Rice flour for dusting

METHOD

- Sieve the rice flour and set aside.

- In a pan, place ½ cup / 100 ml water with 1 tsp oil and ⅛ tsp salt. Cover and bring this mixture to a boil. Uncover, add the rice flour and keep mixing. Turn off the heat after 20 seconds.

- Remove the mixture and place in a kneading plate. Moisten the palm of your hand with room temperature water and knead the dough well. Continue moistening your palm while kneading until the consistency of the dough becomes smooth and soft.

- Divide the dough into 6 equal portions and shape them into round, flat balls.

- Dust your fingers and slightly expand each portion with four fingers. Sprinkle rice flour on a rolling surface and place the extended portion there. Sprinkle a little flour on it and lightly roll with a rolling pin into a 5-inch disc.

- Place a griddle (*tawa*) over medium heat. Carefully lift and place the disc on the griddle. After a minute, flip the disc using a flat spatula. Cook for a minute and flip again. Gently press with a flat spatula until it puffs. Remove and serve hot.

- Repeat the same process to prepare the remaining discs.

PER SERVING	3 PIECES
Calories	136
Fat (grams)	4
Carbohydrates (grams)	24
Protein (grams)	1

- Rice bread can be a substitute for rice and is a good accompaniment for any main dish.

- Cook the breads soon after making the dough, or else the dough loses its texture.

• Shown served with Gravy Button Mushroom (see pg. 126).

SORGHUM FLAT BREAD
Jowar Roti

   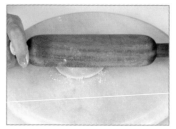

INGREDIENTS

7 Tbsp levelled / 70 gm
sorghum (*jowar*) flour
1/8 tsp Salt
Hot water to prepare
the dough
1 Tbsp /10 gm Sorghum flour
to dust
2 tsp Clarified butter (*ghee*)

METHOD

• Sieve the sorghum flour with salt. Add hot water and knead into
  a soft dough. Keep kneading, adding a little water 3–4 times, until
  the dough feels smooth and shows no cracks on the surface.

• Divide the dough into 4 equal portions. Take one portion and
  slightly knead again, shaping into a round ball. Dust with flour and
  gently flatten while holding between your palm and fingers. Dust
  the rolling board, place the flattened disc, sprinkle a little flour on
  top and gently roll it into a 4-inch disc.

• Brush the disc with a little water. Carefully lift the disc and place
  the moist surface down on a moderately hot griddle (*tawa*).
  Brush the top surface with a little water. After a minute, flip the
  disc using a flat spatula.

• Using a kitchen napkin, press the disc on all sides. Continue
  cooking until a few brown patches are visible. Flip, press again and
  remove from heat.

• Smear ½ tsp clarified butter on top and serve immediately.
  Repeat the same process for the remaining discs.

PER SERVING	2 PIECES
Calories	186
Fat (grams)	6
Carbohydrates (grams)	31.5
Protein (grams)	1.5

• Make the dough just before you plan to prepare the sorghum
  flat bread. The lack of gluten in sorghum does not give this flat
  bread pliability.

• Clarified butter helps for better digestion of the heavy
  sorghum flour.

• Shown served with Fenugreek-Flavoured Yellow Lentil (see pg. 113).

ACCOMPANIMENTS

LEMONGRASS TEA
Nimbu Ghans Chai

INGREDIENTS

3 strands of Lemongrass
2 cups / 400 ml Water
1/8 tsp Ginger (*adrak*), finely chopped

METHOD

• Cut lemongrass into 2-inch-long pieces and set aside.

• Place water in a pan over medium heat. Add the lemongrass pieces and chopped ginger. Bring the mixture to a boil. Simmer for a minute.

• Sieve through a strainer and serve hot.

PER SERVING	1 CUP
Calories	2
Fat (grams)	0
Carbohydrates (grams)	0.5
Protein (grams)	0

• Lemongrass is a good source of iron, which is an essential part of the energy and oxygen-providing ability of red blood cells in the body.

• One stem of lemongrass after cutting gives 30 (2-inch-long) pieces.

DIGESTIVE TEA
Ayurvedic Chai

INGREDIENTS

2 cup / 400 ml Water
2 tsp Fennel (*saunf*) seeds
½ tsp Carom (*ajwain*) seeds
12 (6 + 6) Mint (*pudina*) leaves

METHOD

- In a pan over medium heat, add the water with fennel seeds and carom seeds, and bring the mixture to a boil. Simmer for 1 minute, sieve through a strainer and set the tea aside.

- Add 6 mint leaves in a serving cup, pour the hot tea over the leaves and serve immediately.

PER SERVING	1 CUP
Calories	9.9
Fat (grams)	0
Carbohydrates (grams)	1
Protein (grams)	0

- The cooling effect of mint, along with the digestive properties of both fennel and carom seeds, makes this tea an ideal post-meal beverage.

- Add the fresh mint leaves to the hot tea just before serving to prevent the leaves from browning.

MIXED VEGETABLE YOGHURT
Pachdi Raita

PER SERVING	¾ CUP
Calories	119
Fat (grams)	3
Carbohydrates (grams)	15
Protein (grams)	8

INGREDIENTS

1 cup / 200 gm low-fat
Yoghurt (*dahi*)
Salt, to taste
½ cup / 60 gm Cucumber
(*khira*) peeled, cut into
small pieces
¼ cup / 30 gm Onion (*pyaz*),
finely chopped
¼ cup / 33 gm Tomato
(*tamatar*), cut into small pieces
¼ tsp Green chillies (*hari mirch*),
finely chopped
1 Tbsp fresh Coriander
(*dhaniya*) leaves, finely chopped
¼ tsp roasted Cumin (*bhuna
jeera*) powder (see pg. 222)

METHOD

• In a medium-size bowl, whisk the yoghurt. Add salt to taste, mix and set aside.

• To the whisked yoghurt, add the chopped cucumber, onion, tomato, green chilli and coriander. Mix well, transfer to a serving bowl, garnish with roasted cumin powder and serve chilled.

• Keep any leftovers refrigerated and consume within a day.

• Yoghurt is an excellent source of protein and carbohydrates. It helps to fuel the muscles and keeps one satiated for a longer time.

• For better taste, use fresh yoghurt, as otherwise it may taste sour.

FRESH MINT YOGHURT
Pudina Raita

INGREDIENTS

1 cup / 200 gm low-fat
Yoghurt (*dahi*)
Salt, to taste
½ cup Mint (*pudina*) leaves
¼ tsp roasted Cumin (*bhuna jeera*) powder (see pg. 222),
to garnish

METHOD

• In a medium-size bowl, whisk the yoghurt. Add salt to taste and set aside.

• Grind mint leaves to a smooth paste in a mixer using very little water.

• Mix the mint paste with the whisked yoghurt and transfer to a serving bowl. Garnish with roasted cumin powder and serve chilled.

PER SERVING	¼ CUP
Calories	37
Fat (grams)	1
Carbohydrates (grams)	4
Protein (grams)	3

• Fresh mint contains potassium, an essential mineral for hydration.

• Mix mint paste with yoghurt just before serving, or it may lose its colour and turn to brown.

GOOSEBERRY RELISH
Jhatpat Achari Amla

INGREDIENTS

8 Pieces / 250 gm Gooseberry (*amla*)
2 tsp Mustard oil (*sarson ka tel*)
Pinch, Asafoetida (*hing*)
1/8 tsp Fenugreek seeds (*methi dana*)
1/8 tsp Turmeric (*haldi*) powder
1 tsp Fennel (*saunf*) powder
1 tsp Red chilli (*lal mirch*) powder
Salt, to taste

METHOD

• Wash and steam the gooseberries in a double boiler / vegetable steamer for 12–14 minutes or until the surface is slightly cracked. Remove and set aside to cool at room temperature.

• Remove the seeds and separate the segments.

• In a broad pan over medium heat, heat the oil for 30 seconds. Add the asafoetida, fenugreek seeds, turmeric powder, gooseberry segments, fennel powder, red chilli powder and salt to taste. Mix well. Cook for 2 minutes, stirring constantly. Serve and refrigerate the leftovers.

• Consume within 15 days.

PER SERVING	4 PIECES
Calories	8
Fat (grams)	0
Carbohydrates (grams)	2
Protein (grams)	0

• Gooseberries have multiple health benefits: they are rich in antioxidants, iron, calcium, anthocyanin, flavonoids and potassium.

STAR FRUIT DELIGHT
Kamrak Ki Launji

Serves: 4 (3 cups)
Suggested portion per serving: 3 pieces

INGREDIENTS

250 gm Star fruit (*kamrak*)
2 tsp Mustard oil (*sarson ka tel*)
Pinch, Asafoetida (*hing*)
$1/8$ tsp Fenugreek seeds (*methi dana*)
Salt, to taste
2 tsp Jaggery (*gur*) powder
$1/8$ tsp Red chilli (*lal mirch*) powder
$1/8$ tsp Fennel (*saunf*) powder

METHOD

- Trim both the ends and the spiked edges of the star fruit, cut into $1/4$-inch pieces and remove the seeds. Set aside.

- Heat 2 tsp oil in a non-stick pan for 30 seconds over medium heat. Add the asafoetida, fenugreek, star fruit pieces and salt to taste. Mix and cook for 20 seconds. Reduce the heat, cover and cook for one minute.

- Uncover, add jaggery powder and stir gently.

- Increase to medium heat. Add chilli powder and fennel powder. Mix gently. Remove and serve.

PER SERVING	3 PIECES
Calories	23.2
Fat (grams)	1
Carbohydrates (grams)	2.25
Protein (grams)	1.3

- Star fruit, along with the spices in this recipe, makes this an antioxidant-packed dish.

- This is a seasonal fruit (April–June and October–December) and, therefore, may not be available throughout the year.

GREEN GOOSEBERRY CHUTNEY
Hari Amla Chutney

Serves: As desired (½ cup)
Suggested portion per serving: As desired

PER SERVING	½ CUP
Calories	28
Fat (grams)	0
Carbohydrates (grams)	7
Protein (grams)	0

INGREDIENTS

2 cups tightly packed and fresh
Coriander (*dhaniya*) leaves,
chopped
4 Tbsp Gooseberry (*amla*), cut
into medium cubes
1 tsp Green chillies (*hari mirch*),
finely chopped
Pinch, Asafoetida (*hing*)
Salt, to taste
1–2 tsp Lemon (*nimbu*) juice

METHOD

- In a mixer, grind the coriander leaves, chopped gooseberry, green chilli, asafoetida and salt to taste with very little water. Grind into a fine paste.

- Transfer to a serving bowl. Just before serving, add the lemon juice to taste. Mix well.

- This chutney can be refrigerated for up to 2 days.

- The combination of gooseberry, coriander and lemon makes this chutney power-packed with vitamin C, making it an ideal accompaniment to keep the flu and colds away.

- Add lemon juice in small portions just before serving. If left longer, the chutney may lose its bright colour and turn to a dull green.

ROASTED PEANUT CHUTNEY
Moongphalli Ki Chutney

INGREDIENTS

¼ cup (40 gm) Peanut (*moongphalli*), roasted, skinned (see pg. 211)

¼ cup (25 gm) De-husked, split Bengal gram (*bhuni chana dal*), roasted

1 tsp Green chilli (*hari mirch*), finely chopped

2 tsp fresh Coconut (*nariyal*), grated (see pg. 210)

Salt, to taste

2 Tbsp fresh Coriander (*dhaniya*) leaves, finely chopped

For the tempering:

1 tsp Rice bran oil

⅛ tsp Mustard (*sarson*) seeds

10 Curry leaves (*kadhipatta*)

1 dry Red chilli (*sookhi lal mirch*), broken into 2 pieces

METHOD

- In a mixer, grind the peanuts, Bengal gram, green chilli, coconut and salt to taste. Add sufficient water to make a smooth paste.

- Add the chopped coriander and pulse for a few seconds more to shred the leaves.

- Transfer into a serving bowl.

- **For the tempering**, heat the oil in a tempering ladle for 20 seconds over medium heat. Add the mustard seeds and, when they splutter, add curry leaves and red chilli. Pour immediately over the chutney and serve.

PER SERVING	1 TBSP
Calories	71
Fat (grams)	4.3
Carbohydrates (grams)	5
Protein (grams)	3

- Peanuts and coconut are an excellent source of fats and ensure that fat-soluble vitamins, such as B vitamins, are absorbed by the body.

INDIAN FETA CHEESE
Desi Paneer Mein Videshi Tadka

INGREDIENTS

2½ cups / 500 ml low-fat Milk
1–2 Tbsp White vinegar
(*safed sirka*)
2 tsp Hung yoghurt (*chakka*)
(see pg. 207)
Pinch, salt
$\frac{1}{8}$ tsp Mustard (*sarson*) powder
2 tsp Celery, finely chopped
(see pg. 216)

PER SERVING	25 GM
Calories	350
Fat (grams)	5
Carbohydrates (grams)	32
Protein (grams)	20

METHOD

• Bring milk to a boil in a pan over medium heat. Turn off the heat. Gradually add the white vinegar and stir until the milk curdles (see pg. 206).

• Let it stand for 2 minutes and then drain in a cloth sieve/muslin cloth. Fold the cloth over the cottage cheese while moulding into a square. Place a heavy weight over it and leave for 20 minutes. Gently unwrap the cottage cheese.

• In a mixer, grind the cottage cheese with thick yoghurt, salt and mustard powder into a fine paste. Add the chopped celery, mix and remove onto a flat plate, forming a square shape. Refrigerate for 2 hours.

• Cut into ½-inch square pieces and refrigerate. Use as per recipe or as desired.

• Feta cheese is originally from Greece and is traditionally made with sheep or goat's milk.

• Unlike regular feta cheese, which is crumbly with a grainy texture, this recipe makes a very soft and creamy-textured version of it. Enjoy it spread on gluten-free toasted bread.

YOGHURT-MUSTARD SAUCE
Sarson Chutney

PER SERVING	1 TBSP
Calories	20
Fat (grams)	0.8
Carbohydrates (grams)	2
Protein (grams)	1.2

INGREDIENTS

½ cup / 100 gm low-fat
Yoghurt (*dahi*)
1 tsp Mustard (*sarson*) powder
¼ tsp Red chilli (*lal mirch*) flakes
⅛ tsp Salt

METHOD

• Whisk the yoghurt well. Add the mustard powder, red chilli flakes and salt. Mix well.

• Transfer into a serving bowl and serve.

• A perfect accompaniment for a meal on a hot summer day, yoghurt provides a good balance of protein, which keeps the stomach full, and carbohydrates that fuel the brain and muscles.

• For the dip, ½ tsp readymade mustard sauce can be used instead of the mustard powder.

LEMON-FLAVOURED MANGO GINGER
Tazi Aamba Haldi

 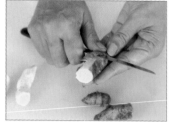  

INGREDIENTS

1 tsp Fennel (*saunf*) seeds
100 gm Mango ginger (*aamba haldi*)
30 gm Green chillies (*hari mirch*)
1/3 tsp Salt
3 tsp Lemon (*nimbu*) juice

METHOD

- Using a mortar and pestle, pound the fennel seeds to a coarse powder. Set aside.

- Peel and julienne the mango ginger into thin 1-inch-long pieces and set aside.

- Slit green chillies and cut into thin 1½-inch-long pieces and set aside.

- Combine the mango ginger, green chilli, fennel powder, salt and lemon juice. Serve.

- This can be refrigerated for up to a week.

PER SERVING	2 TSP
Calories	58
Fat (grams)	0
Carbohydrates (grams)	4
Protein (grams)	0

- The anti-nausea and anti-pyretic effects of mango ginger create an ideal accompaniment for pregnant women suffering from morning sickness.

TANGY TURMERIC ROOT
Khatti Kachchi Haldi

INGREDIENTS
100 gm Fresh turmeric root
(*kachchi haldi*)
½ tsp Salt
2 tsp Lemon (*nimbu*) juice

METHOD
- Peel and cut the turmeric root into thin, round discs. Add the salt and lemon juice. Mix well.

- Keep aside for 30 minutes before serving.

- Refrigerate any leftovers for up to 15 days.

PER SERVING	¹/₃ CUP
Calories	18
Fat (grams)	0.3
Carbohydrates (grams)	3.5
Protein (grams)	0.3

- Turmeric has a very strong anti-inflammatory effect, which can be extremely beneficial for stomach ailments such as Crohn's disease.

- In India, turmeric root is available during the winter season.

POINTED GOURD MASH
Parwal Bharta

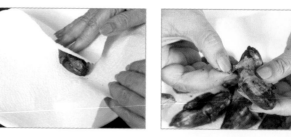

INGREDIENTS

6 / 200 gm medium Pointed
gourd (*parwal*)
½ tsp Rice bran oil
⅓ cup / 60 gm Onion (*pyaz*),
finely chopped (see pg. 215)
½ tsp Green chillies (*hari mirch*),
finely chopped
2 tsp fresh Coriander (*dhaniya*)
leaves, finely chopped
Salt, to taste
1 tsp Lemon (*nimbu*) juice

METHOD

• Place the pointed gourd on a chopping board. Make a slit in the centre of each one of them, keeping the shape intact.

• Brush the surface of the pointed gourd with oil.

• Pierce with a fork and roast over an open flame until the skin is charred and wrinkled. Immediately wrap in a kitchen towel and cover with a bowl. Set aside for 20 minutes. Unwrap, peel and mash the pointed gourd using a masher.

• Just before serving, combine the mashed pointed gourd with chopped onions, green chillies, coriander, salt and lemon juice.

PER SERVING	1 TBSP
Calories	16
Fat (grams)	0
Carbohydrates (grams)	3
Protein (grams)	1

• Roasting the pointed gourd helps retain all its goodness and nutrients – besides giving it a lovely, nutty taste.

SPINACH YOGHURT
Palak Raita

INGREDIENTS

1½ / 98 gm tightly packed
Spinach (*palak*), washed, dried
over the kitchen towel, chopped
1cup / 200 gm low-fat
Yoghurt (*dahi*)
Salt, to taste
1 Tbsp / 15 ml low-fat Milk
⅛ tsp Red chilli (*lal mirch*)
powder, to garnish
¼ tsp roasted Cumin (*bhuna
jeera*) powder (see pg. 222),
to garnish

METHOD

- Steam the chopped spinach in a double boiler / vegetable steamer for 1½ minutes (see pgs. 218–19). Remove and set aside to cool.

- Whisk the yoghurt, add salt to taste and set aside.

- Grind the steamed spinach with 1 Tbsp milk in a mixer to a coarse paste. Set aside.

- Mix the ground spinach paste with the whisked yoghurt and transfer to a serving bowl. Garnish with roasted cumin powder and red chilli powder. Serve chilled.

- Refrigerate any leftovers for up to a day.

PER SERVING	½ CUP
Calories	59
Fat (grams)	1
Carbohydrates (grams)	7
Protein (grams)	5

- The simple carbohydrates and protein derived from the yoghurt, along with the fibre from the spinach, make this a well-balanced accompaniment to any meal.

- Mix the ground spinach with the whisked yoghurt just before serving to retain its fresh green colour.

TOMATO RELISH
Tamatar Ki Chutney

INGREDIENTS
1 tsp Rice bran oil
Pinch, Asafoetida (hing)
⅛ tsp Cumin (jeera) seeds
1 medium / 75 gm Onion (pyaz), peeled, cut into medium cubes (see pg. 215)
1 tsp Ginger (adrak), finely chopped
½ tsp Green chillies (hari mirch), finely chopped
¼ tsp Red chilli (lal mirch) powder
4 medium / 375 gm Tomatoes (tamatar), roasted, peeled, cut into medium cubes (see pg. 224)
2 Tbsp Water
Salt, to taste
2 tsp fresh Coriander (dhaniya) leaves, finely chopped, to garnish

METHOD
- Heat 1 tsp oil in a pan for 30 seconds over medium heat. Add the asafoetida, cumin seeds, onion, ginger and green chilli, and sauté over medium heat for a minute. Add the chilli powder, tomatoes, water and salt to taste.

- Mash well with a masher, reduce the heat and cook until the mixture is semi-thick.

- Garnish with fresh coriander. Mix and serve.

PER SERVING	2 TBSP
Calories	16
Fat (grams)	0
Carbohydrates (grams)	3
Protein (grams)	1

- Tomatoes are a good source of lycopene, a powerful antioxidant beneficial for maintenance of good vision, prevention of heart disease and possibly reducing the risk of Alzheimer's.

TRICOLOUR STUFFED OKRA
Tirangi Bhindi

Serves: 3 (12 pieces)
Suggested portion per serving: 4 pieces

INGREDIENTS

12 / 55 gm tender, medium
Okra (*bhindi*)
1½ Tbsp / 30 gm Onion (*pyaz*),
finely chopped
1½ Tbsp / 70 gm Tomatoes
(*tamatar*), finely chopped
1½ Tbsp / 50 gm Cucumber
(*khira*), finely chopped
Salt, to taste
¼ tsp *Chaat masala*
2 tsp fresh Coriander (*dhaniya*)
leaves, finely chopped
A few drops of lemon juice

METHOD

• Trim both the ends of the okra. Slit vertically with a sharp knife, keeping the vegetable intact.

• Steam the okra in a double boiler / vegetable steamer for 3 minutes. Remove and set aside to cool.

• Mix the chopped onion, tomatoes, cucumber, salt, *chaat masala*, fresh coriander and lemon juice. Stuff this filling into the steamed okra evenly and serve.

PER SERVING	4 PIECES
Calories	8
Fat (grams)	0
Carbohydrates (grams)	2
Protein (grams)	0

• Okra is packed with valuable nutrients like sodium and potassium, which help in proper muscle contraction in the body, thus avoiding cramps.

TANGY DATE CHUTNEY
Khajoorki Saunth

INGREDIENTS

100 gm soft Dates (*khajoor*), washed

3½ tsp Mango powder (*amchur*)

2¾ cups / 550 ml (2¼ + ½) Water

¼ tsp Black salt (*kala namak*)

¼ tsp Spice mix (*garam masala*) (see pg. 222)

½ tsp roasted Cumin (*bhuna jeera*) powder (see pg. 222)

For the Masala:

Pinch, Asafoetida (*hing*)

½ tsp Coriander (*dhaniya*) powder

½ tsp Red chilli (*lal mirch*) powder

METHOD

- In a pan over medium heat, add the washed dates with 2¼ cups / 450 ml water and bring the mixture to a boil. Simmer for 2 minutes and leave to cool at room temperature. Set aside.

- Reserve the water for later use. Remove the seed of each date. Set aside.

- Blend the dates with the reserved water in a mixer to a smooth paste and strain through a sieve. Set aside.

- In a pan, mix mango powder with the remaining water, sieved date mixture and black salt. Bring this mixture to a boil, stirring occasionally. Simmer for 15 minutes or until the mixture is semi-thick. Set aside to cool.

- In a flat pan over medium heat, dry roast the Masala ingredients, stirring frequently until light golden brown. Set aside.

- Add the *garam masala*, roasted cumin and the dry roast Masala ingredients to the cooked mixture. Mix well and serve.

- Refrigerate any leftovers and consume within 15 days.

PER SERVING	1½ TBSP
Calories	48
Fat (grams)	0
Carbohydrates (grams)	12
Protein (grams)	0

- Dates are a great source of fibre. However, they must be consumed with a good amount of fluid in order to aid in digestion.

- This chutney has a special place in Indian kitchens, with the mango powder giving an extra tartness to this accompaniment.

DESSERTS

BARNYARD MILLET MANGO PUDDING
Samak Aur Aam Ki Kheer

INGREDIENTS

1½ Tbsp / 22 gm Barnyard
millet (*samak ke chawal*)
1½ cups / 300 ml low-fat Milk
¾ tsp Rose water
1 cup / 160 gm chilled Mango
(*aam*), cut into small cubes
2 tsp Pistachio (*pista*), slivered
(see pg. 208), to garnish

METHOD

- Wash the barnyard millet in water. Drain and set aside.

- In a heavy-bottom wok (*kadhai*), bring the milk to a boil over medium heat, stirring frequently. Add the barnyard millet to the boiling milk and bring the mixture to a boil. Continue cooking over low heat for five minutes or until the mixture is semi-thick. Turn off the heat and set aside to cool. Refrigerate until chilled.

- Just before serving, add rose water and chopped mangoes to the barnyard millet mixture and mix gently.

- Serve chilled, garnished with slivered pistachios.

PER SERVING	½ CUP
Calories	264
Fat (grams)	4
Carbohydrates (grams)	49
Protein (grams)	8

- The combination of the protein-heavy barnyard millet and energy-filled mango makes this an ideal dessert that doesn't cause a spike in blood sugar levels.

- Barnyard millet has a tendency to thicken after it cools down. Therefore adhere to the cooking time mentioned.

CANDIED AMARANTH
Ramdana Laddu

INGREDIENTS

100 gm Amaranth (*ramdana*)
seeds
80 gm Jaggery (*gur*) powder
¼ cup / 50 ml Water

METHOD

• Heat a pan over medium heat until very hot. Add 1 tsp of
  amaranth seeds and swirl the seeds around with the help of
  a kitchen towel until the seeds pop like popcorn. Repeat the
  process to pop the remaining seeds in batches. Sieve the seeds,
  discarding the ones that have not popped.

• In a broad pan, add jaggery powder and ¼ cup / 50 ml of water.
  Bring this mixture to a boil over low heat, stirring occasionally
  until the jaggery mixture / syrup reaches one-string consistency.
  Turn off the heat.

• Immediately add the popped amaranth seeds and mix
  continuously with both hands, using spatulas, to create a light and
  airy mixture.

• While the mixture is hot, apply a little water on the palm of your
  hand. Take a small portion of the mixture and press with both
  hands to form round balls. Repeat until you have 15 balls. Cool
  and serve.

• Store in an air-tight jar and consume within a week.

PER SERVING	1 PIECE
Calories	177.3
Fat (grams)	5.7
Carbohydrates (grams)	13
Protein (grams)	3.5

• Amaranth contains a good amount of magnesium and calcium,
  making this dish a nutritious treat for growing children.

• The consistency of the jaggery syrup is important to bind the
  Candied Amaranth. Be quick in forming the balls as a cold mixture
  does not bind.

- Amaranth is also known as *rajgira* in Hindi.

CARROT DELIGHT
Gajar Ki Kheer

INGREDIENTS

¼ cup / 35 gm Black raisins (*kali kishmish*)

½ kg Red carrots (*lal gajar*)

5 cups / 1 L low-fat Milk

1 Tbsp Honey

2 Green cardamom (*choti elaichi*), seeds only, powdered (see pg. 209)

12 Almonds (*badam*), slivered (see pg. 208), to garnish

METHOD

• Wash the black raisins in 1 cup / 200 ml water. Drain and set aside.

• Peel and grate the carrots. Set aside.

• Place the grated carrots in a heavy-bottom wok (*kadhai*). Cook over medium heat, stirring frequently for 2 minutes.

• Add milk and bring the mixture to a boil. Continue cooking over low heat until the mixture is reduced to ⅓ of its original quantity, stirring occasionally.

• Add the honey and raisins. Stir and bring the mixture to a boil over medium heat. Lower the heat and simmer for 2 minutes.

• Add the cardamom powder and mix. Turn off the heat and set aside to cool.

• Serve warm or cold, as desired. Garnish with slivered almonds.

PER SERVING	½ CUP
Calories	148
Fat (grams)	4
Carbohydrates (grams)	20
Protein (grams)	8

• Carrots are an excellent source of beta carotene, which helps maintain good eye health.

• Red carrots are seasonal and can be replaced with orange carrots. You may want to increase the quantity of honey if using orange carrots, as they are less sweet than red carrots.

FINGER MILLET BITES
Ragi Meeng Paag

INGREDIENTS

2 tsp levelled Flax seeds (*alsi ke beej*)
2 tsp Musk melon seeds (*kharbooje ke beej*)
2 tsp Clarified butter (*ghee*)
4 Tbsp / 50 gm slightly heaped Finger millet (*ragi*) flour
3 Tbsp / 30 gm levelled Jaggery (*gur*), powdered
¼ cup / 50 ml Water

METHOD

• Place flax seeds in a pan over medium heat. Stir frequently until the seeds start to crackle. Turn off the heat. Cool and grind coarsely. Set aside.

• Place musk melon seeds in a pan and roast over medium heat. Stir constantly until the seeds crackle and turn light brown. Set aside.

• Heat clarified butter in a flat pan over medium heat and mix in the finger millet flour. Lower the heat and stir constantly until you get a roasted aroma and the flour turns a darker shade (approximately 8–10 minutes). Remove and set aside to cool.

• In a plate, mix the roasted finger millet, musk melon seeds and ground flax seeds. Set aside this *ragi* mixture.

• In a pan, add the jaggery powder with ¼ cup / 50 ml water. Bring this mixture to a boil over low heat, stirring frequently, until the jaggery mixture / syrup reaches one-string consistency. Turn off the heat.

• Immediately add the jaggery syrup to the *ragi* mixture. Divide the mixture and fill into chocolate / cake moulds that are around ¾-inch x ¾-inch. Press firmly on top to set well.

• Cool and remove the finger millet bites from the moulds and serve.

PER SERVING	2 PIECES
Calories	59.5
Fat (grams)	2.3
Carbohydrates (grams)	9
Protein (grams)	0.7

• The outer coverings of flax seeds are extremely difficult to digest; therefore, it is recommended to grind the seeds to gain maximum nutritional benefits.

• Be careful when making one-string consistency of jaggery as overcooking will cause the bites to become very hard in texture.

JAGGERY-COATED SWEET POTATO
Meethi Shakarkandi

INGREDIENTS

500 gm Sweet potatoes
(*shakarkandi*)
3 tsp (1 + 2) cold pressed
Coconut oil (*nariyal tel*)
50 gm Jaggery (*gur*), powdered
¼ cup / 50 ml Water
12 Almonds (*badam*), slivered,
roasted (see pg. 208), to garnish

METHOD

• Pre-heat the oven to 200°C.

• Wash and pat dry the sweet potatoes with a kitchen towel. Apply 1 tsp oil on the surface of the sweet potatoes. Bake in the pre-heated oven for 15–25 minutes or until cooked through. Avoid over-baking of sweet potato as it dries it out, hence making it brittle and difficult to cut into discs.

• Cool at room temperature. Peel the sweet potato, discard the pointed ends and cut into ¼-inch discs. Set aside.

• Heat a broad non-stick pan for 30 seconds over medium heat. Brush the pan with ½ tsp coconut oil and place half the sweet potato discs on it. Brush the tops of the discs with ½ tsp oil. Cook over medium heat, turning occasionally, until the discs turn light golden brown on both sides. Remove and repeat the same process with the remaining discs using the same amount of oil.

• Place all the cooked sweet potato discs in a broad, heavy-bottom pan. Add jaggery powder and ¼ cup / 50 ml water. Cook over medium heat while turning gently. Cook until the water evaporates and the discs are coated evenly with jaggery.

• Garnish with roasted almonds and serve hot.

PER SERVING	½ CUP
Calories	138
Fat (grams)	2
Carbohydrates (grams)	27
Protein (grams)	3

• The cold press process in coconut oil extraction helps keep the nutritional value of the oil intact. Although coconut is classified as a fat, it can also act as a carbohydrate, providing fuel to the body.

• Use sweet potatoes with medium thickness as they are more flavourful.

PALM JAGGERY RICE
Gud Ke Chawal

INGREDIENTS

5 cups / 1 L Water

½ cup / 90 gm Basmati rice, washed, soaked in water for 30 minutes, drained in a colander

100 gm Palm jaggery (*gur*), powdered

¼ tsp Red chilli (*lal mirch*) flakes

⅛ tsp Salt

1 tsp Lemon (*nimbu*) juice

¼ tsp Lemon rind

2 tsp Clarified butter (*ghee*)

2 Tbsp Pine nuts (*chilgoza*)

10 Almonds (*badam*), slivered (see pg. 208), to garnish

2 tsp Pistachio (*pista*), slivered (see pg. 208), to garnish

METHOD

- Boil 5 cups / 1 L water in a pan. Add the soaked rice and bring to a boil. Cover and cook over low heat until the rice is soft and the grains are intact. Drain and set aside.

- Place half of the cooked rice in a flat cooking pan. Add jaggery powder, chilli flakes, salt, lemon juice, lemon rind and clarified butter. Spread the remaining cooked rice evenly on top. Cover with a lid and let it remain for 5 minutes.

- Uncover the pan and mix the rice mixture gently. It will release water. Cook over medium heat for a minute. Turn off the heat. Cover the pan and let the rice sit for 10 minutes.

- Repeat this process three more times or until all the water evaporates. Add pine nuts and mix. Serve garnished with almonds and pistachio.

PER SERVING	⅓ CUP
Calories	185
Fat (grams)	5
Carbohydrates (grams)	30
Protein (grams)	5

- Palm jaggery is a good substitute for sugar as it contains small amounts of B vitamins and zinc, which help build energy and immunity.

COOKING PROCESSES

WORKING WITH DAIRY

COTTAGE CHEESE / *PANEER*

- Over medium heat, bring 5 cups (1 L) of low-fat milk to a boil in a pan. Turn off the heat and add 1–2 Tbsp of lemon juice. Gradually stir until the milk curdles.

- Let it stand for 2 minutes.

- Drain in a cloth sieve / muslin cloth.

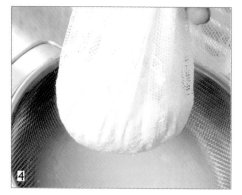

- Bunch the ends of the cloth and lift, let it stand in a colander for 5 minutes and discard the whey.

GRATE AND MASH

- Hand-grate the hung cottage cheese.

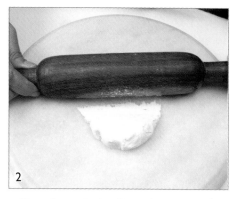

- Place the grated cottage cheese on a flat surface and mash to a smooth paste with a rolling pin. Use as per recipe.

TIP:
- 5 cups (1 L) of milk makes 125 gms of cottage cheese (*paneer*).
- To obtain soft cottage cheese: Turn the heat off immediately after the milk comes to a boil. After placing in a muslin cloth, do not squeeze as the whey drains away naturally.

SETTING YOGHURT / *DAHI*

- Heat 5 cups (1 L) of low-fat milk until lukewarm (40°–45°C).

- Place ½ tsp yoghurt culture in a bowl.

- Pour in the lukewarm milk and mix well.

- Cover and keep in a warm place for 3–6 hours or until it sets.

MAKING HUNG YOGHURT / *CHAKKA*

- Place 2 cups (400 gm) yoghurt in a sieve and leave for 3–4 hours. Discard the whey and use as per the recipe.

TIP:

Setting Yoghurt (*dahi*)
- Do not use hot milk to set yoghurt as this will alter its taste and texture.
- Yoghurt usually sets faster during summer, compared to winter.
- After setting, yoghurt needs to be refrigerated to prevent souring.

Making Hung Yoghurt (*chakka*)
- 2 cups (400 gm) of yoghurt will make 1 cup (100 gm) of hung yoghurt.

WORKING WITH DRY FRUIT

ALMONDS / *BADAM*

- With a sharp knife, cut the almonds into 3 pieces. Cover and refrigerate. Consume within 7 days.

ROASTING OF ALMONDS / *BADAM*

- Place slivered almonds in a baking tray.

SLIVERING PISTACHIOS / *PISTA*

- Finely slice the whole pistachio with a sharp knife. Cover and refrigerate. Consume within 7 days.

SLIVERING ALMONDS / *BADAM*

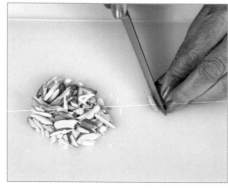

- Finely slice the whole almond with a sharp knife. Cover and refrigerate. Consume within 7 days.

- Pre-heat the oven at 180°C. Roast the slivered almonds for 2–4 minutes or until light golden brown.

TIP:
- Almonds (*badam*) and pistachios (*pista*) are often used to lend flavour and texture to Indian desserts.

CARDAMOM POWDER / *CHOTI ELAICHI*

- Place the seeds of green cardamom pods in a mortar.
- Grind the seeds with a pestle.
- Pound into a fine powder.

CHOPPING OF DATES / *KHAJOOR*

- Slit the date vertically. Remove the seed.
- Cut thin slices lengthwise.
- Chop the slices as per recipe requirement.

ROASTING AND GRINDING OF FLAX SEEDS / *ALSI KE BEEJ*

- Place 2 tsp flax seeds in a pan over heat, and stir frequently until the seeds start to crackle. Turn off the heat and cool.
- Grind coarsely and use as per recipe.

TIP

- Cardamom (*choti elaichi*) powder can be refrigerated in an air-tight container for one week.

WORKING WITH FRUIT

AVOCADO / *MAKHAN FAL*

1

2

3

- Use a sharp knife to cut the avocado in half lengthwise until you feel the knife hit the pit. Rotate and twist with both hands and gently pull them part.

- Remove the pit.

- Scoop out the pulp.

POMELO / *CHAKOTARA*

1

2

3

- Make a few 1-inch-deep slits in the spongy pomelo skin. Peel the skin.

- Remove the fruit.

- Remove the membrane and seeds.
- Cut into desired pieces.

COCONUT / *NARIYAL*

1

2

- Break open the coconut and remove the flesh with a sturdy, sharp knife. Peel off the dark brown skin.

- Grate the white flesh and use as per recipe.

TIP:

Avocado (*makhan fal*):
- The avocado has a short shelf life. It oxidizes after cutting, changing colour to pale brown. Consume fresh.

Pomelo (*chakotara*):
- It is a seasonal fruit, and so not available throughout the year.

Coconut (*nariyal*):
- Due to a short shelf life, keep it refrigerated. Consume within 2 days.

ROASTING WITH SELECT INGREDIENTS

AMARANTH SEEDS / *RAMDANA*

- Heat pan until very hot. Add Amaranth seeds.

- Rotate with the help of a kitchen napkin until the seeds pop.

- Sieve the popped seeds and discard the unpopped ones.

SESAME SEEDS / *TIL*

- Add ½ tsp sesame seeds into a pan. Dry roast over low heat until light golden brown. Stir frequently.

- Cool and grind in a mixer / food processor. Remove.

PEANUTS / *MOONGPHALLI*

- Place ½ cup peanuts in a baking tray and bake in a pre-heated oven at 140°C for 5–8 minutes, mixing in-between.

- Remove and cool, then skin the peanuts by hand.

TIP
- Only add 2 tsps of Amaranth seeds at a time as they splutter quickly.
- Refrigerate skinned peanuts in an air-tight jar. Consume within 15 days.

MAKING FRESH COOKING PASTE

GINGER / *ADRAK* (MAKES 2 TSP)

1

- Place 2 tsp of chopped ginger in a mortar.

2

- Pound to a fine paste with a pestle.

3

- Use the fresh paste as required.

GREEN CHILLI / *HARI MIRCH* (MAKES 2 TSP)

1

- Place 2 tsp of chopped green chillies in a mortar.

2

- Pound to a fine paste with a pestle.

3

- Use the fresh paste as required.

GARLIC / *LASAN* (MAKES 2 TSP)

1

- Place 16 peeled garlic cloves in a mortar.

2

- Pound to a fine paste with a pestle.

3

- Use the fresh paste as required.

PRESSURE COOKING

GREEN BANANA / *KACHA KELA*

- Place the cooking rack inside the pressure cooker. Add 1½ cups / 300 ml of water into the pressure cooker.

- Place the plantains on the cooking rack and close the lid. Pressure cook over high heat to one whistle. Simmer for 4 minutes.

- Turn off the heat and let the pressure release. Remove, peel and use as per recipe.

LOTUS STEM / *KAMAL KAKDI*

COLOCASIA / *ARVI*

- Add 1½ cups / 300 ml of water into the pressure cooker.
- Place the cooking rack inside the pressure cooker. Place the colander with the lotus stem pieces on top of the cooking rack.
- Pressure cook over high heat to one whistle and simmer as per recipe requirement.
- Turn off the heat and let the pressure settle.

- Add 1½ cups / 300 ml of water into the pressure cooker.
- Place the cooking rack inside the pressure cooker. Place the colander with the colocasia on top of the cooking rack.
- Pressure cook over high heat to one whistle, simmer for 4 minutes.
- Turn off the heat and let the pressure settle. Remove, peel, use as per recipe.

TIP:
- Pressure cooking vegetables over a cooking rack with minimum water keeps their nutritional value intact.
- If you don't have a pressure coooker, boil in a conventional pot until tender. Increase the cooking time and add more water if necessary.

WORKING WITH VEGETABLES

BEANS / *PHALI*

- String the beans and cut into slant pieces.

BROCCOLI

- Remove the florets and cut into 1-inch size.

LOTUS STEM / *KAMAL KAKDI*

- Peel and cut the lotus stem into slant pieces.

CARROT / *GAJAR*

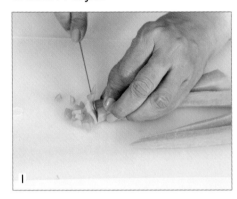

1

2

- Cut each carrot horizontally into half. Slit the half carrot vertically into thin strips. Bundle the strips and chop them into pieces as per recipe requirement.

- Peel and cut each carrot into $1/8$-inch slant pieces. Julienne each slant piece.

DRUMSTICK

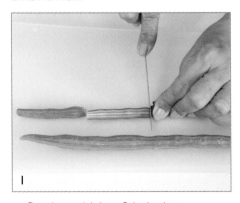

1

2

- Cut drumstick into 2-inch pieces.

- String each piece from all sides.

ONION / *PYAZ*

1

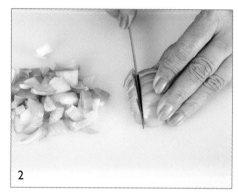

2

- Peel and cut onion into half, cut each half portion of onion into ¼ or ⅛-inch lengthwise and then cut into small pieces.

- Cut into medium cubes.

ZUCCHINI

1

2

- Cut zucchini into ¼-inch slant pieces, as per the recipe.

- Cut each piece lengthwise into desired thickness.

TIP:
- While buying lotus stems, select the ones with closed ends as the open ended ones are muddy inside.
- For better taste, choose drumsticks that are not too hard and rigid.

WORKING WITH LEAFY GREENS

CELERY

1

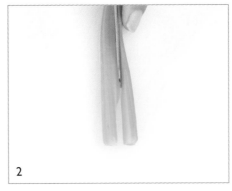

2

3

- Using a sharp knife, remove the stringy portions of the celery stalk.

- Slice the stalk lengthwise into desired thickness.

- Cut as per recipe requirement.

FENUGREEK / *METHI*

- Wash and cut the tender stalk and leaves as required by the recipe.

SPINACH / *PALAK*

- Wash and cut the tender stalk and leaves as required by the recipe.

CORIANDER / *DHANIYA*

- Wash and cut the tender stalk and leaves as required by the recipe.

SPRING ONION / *HARA PYAZ*

- Wash and cut the tender stalk and leaves as required by the recipe.

TIP:
- While ready-made pastes are available, freshly-made pastes lend the best flavour and aroma to the dish.

MAKING SPROUTS

WHOLE GREEN GRAM SPROUTS / *ANKURIT SABUT MOONG*

1

2

3

- Soak ½ cup of whole green gram lentil for 10 hours.

- Drain the water and place in a sprout farm container.

- Add ½ cup / 100ml water.

4

5

TIP:
- Follow the same process for other grains also.
- Sprouting will take 3–4 days for methi, moth bean and whole black chickpea sprouts. Weather conditions can affect sprouting times.

- Cover with a lid. Keep adding ½ cup / 100ml water every 8 hours until the sprouts are formed.

- Sprouts should be ready in 1–2 days.

FENUGREEK SPROUTS / *ANKURIT METHI*

MOTH BEAN SPROUTS / *ANKURIT MOTH*

WHOLE BLACK CHICKPEA SPROUTS / *ANKURIT KALA CHANNA*

GOOSEFOOT LEAVES / *BATHUA*

- Add 2 cups / 400 ml water in a broad vessel and bring to a boil.

- Place chopped goosefoot leaves in a colander over boiling water.

- Cover with a lid and steam for 1½ minutes.

- Uncover and remove the cooked goosefoot leaves. Use as per recipe.

GREEN BANANA / *KACHA KELA*

TIP:
- Goosefoot is a versatile plant available in abundance during winter months. It has a unique taste, along with high nutrition value.
- Cooking time should be followed as per recipe requirement, and should be monitored after placing the colander over boiling water.

GREEN PEAS / *HARA MATAR*

BROCCOLI

BITTER GOURD / *KARELA*

WHOLE BLACK CHICKPEA SPROUTS / *ANKURIT KALA CHANNA*

TIP:
• Follow the same steaming process as per goosefoot leaves.
• Water is sprinkled over cooked peas to retain their original green colour.

WORKING WITH RICE

COOKING BROWN RICE

- Wash and soak 1 cup / 175 gm brown rice in 4 cups / 800 ml water for 30 minutes and drain.

- Boil 6½ cups / 1.3 L of water and add the soaked rice. Bring to a boil and cook covered over low heat, until the rice is soft but firm.

- Drain in a colander and use as per the recipe.

COOKING BLACK RICE

- Wash and soak ½ cup / 90 gm black / red rice in plenty of water for 30 minutes and drain.

- Boil 1 cup / 200 ml of water in a broad pan, add the soaked rice and bring to a boil.

- Cover the pan and simmer for 20–30 minutes or until the rice is cooked through.

COOKING RED RICE

- Follow the same quantity and process as black rice.

TIP:
- The cook time will vary depending on the variety of rice.
- To check if the rice is completely cooked, place a few grains of cooked rice on a plate and press with your index finger to check the texture.
- 1 cup of raw rice will make about 3 cups of cooked rice.

WORKING WITH STAPLES

BARNYARD MILLET / *SAMAK KE CHAWAL*

- Wash and soak ¼ cup / 50 gms barnyard millet in plenty of water for 15 minutes and drain. Place 4 cups / 800 ml water in a pan and bring to a boil. Add barnyard millet and cook for 1 minute.

- Immediately drain using a micro sieve and add 1 tsp oil.

- Keep mixing gently until the millet cools to room temperature.

QUINOA

- Wash and soak ½ cup / 80 gms quinoa in plenty of water for 30 minutes and drain.

- Boil ¾ cup / 150ml of water in a broad pan, add the soaked quinoa and bring to a boil. Cover the pan with a lid.

- Cook over low heat for 15–20 minutes or until the water evaporates.

TIP:
- Follow the proper cooking time for barnyard millet as otherwise it has a tendency to become lumpy.

SPICES & SPICE MIXES

CHAAT MASALA

- Dry roast 1 tbsp cumin (*jeera*) seeds and ¾ tbsp fennel seeds in a pan over low heat until light golden brown, stirring frequently.

- Cool and grind to a fine powder. Mix with 1 tbsp mango powder, 1 tbsp black salt, 1 tsp red chilli powder, ½ tsp mint powder and ¼ tsp ginger powder.

- Store in an air-tight jar.

ROASTED CUMIN POWDER / *BHUNA JEERA*

- Dry roast 2 tbsp cumin seeds in a pan over low heat, stirring frequently until light golden brown.

- Cool, grind coarsely and store in an air-tight jar.

SPICE MIX / *GARAM MASALA*

- Place 2 tbsp black peppercorn, seeds of 8 black cardamoms and 2 tsp cloves in a mixer / food processor.

- Grind to a fine powder and store in an air-tight jar.

SPICY LENTIL RICE – SPICE MIX / *BISI BELE MASALA*

- Dry roast ½ tsp de-husked and split Bengal gram (*chana dal*), ½ tsp de-husked and split black gram (*dhuli urad dal*), ¹/₈ tsp fenugreek seeds (*methi dana*), 1 dry red chilli (*sookhi lal mirch*), 2 tsp coriander (*dhaniya*) seeds, ¾ tsp cumin (*jeera*) seeds and ½ tsp poppy (*khus khus*) seeds in a pan over low heat until light golden brown, stirring frequently.
- Cool and grind to a slightly coarse powder.
- Use as per recipe.

SAMBHAR POWDER

- Dry roast 2 Tbps coriander (*dhaniya*) seeds, 2 tsp cumin (*jeera*) seeds, ¼ tsp fenugreek seeds (*methi dana*), 4 dry red chillies (*sookhi lal mirch*) and 1 Tbsp de-husked, split Bengal gram (*chana dal*) in a pan over low heat until light golden brown, stirring frequently.
- Cool and grind to a slightly coarse powder.
- Use as per recipe.

TIP:
- Although these spices and spice mixes are available readymade in supermarkets, their aromas and flavours are best when freshly made.
- Freshly-made spices may be stored for 2–4 weeks with no significant loss of aroma.

WORKING WITH TOMATOES

ROASTING TOMATOES / *TAMATAR*

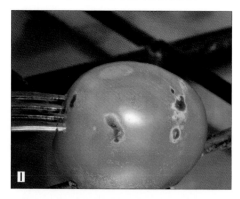

1

- Pierce the head of the tomato with a fork and roast over an open flame until the skin is slightly charred and wrinkled.

2

- Cool and peel the skin.

3

- Cut as per the recipe requirement.

GRATING TOMATOES

1

- Halve the tomato lengthwise. Grate from the cut side down until reaching the skin.

2

- Once grated, use as per the recipe.

CHOPPING TOMATOES

- Halve the tomato lengthwise. Cut into ¼-inch strips. Cut the strips into cubes as per recipe requirement.

TIP:
- Always use firm, plump, red tomatoes for better taste.

LIQUIDIZED TOMATOES

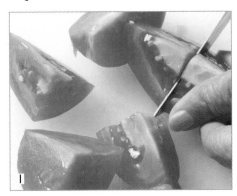

- Cut the tomatoes into 8 pieces.

- Blend in a blender / food processor.

- Blend until it is a smooth liquid.

TOMATO MASALA

- Heat pan. Add $1/8$ tsp rice bran oil, $1/8$ tsp red chilli powder and 2 medium tomatoes, grated.

- Add salt to taste.

- Cook over medium heat until it thickens.

TIP:
- Use the tomato quantity and tomato masala mixture as per recipe requirement.

MISCELLANEOUS

ALMOND MILK / *BADAM DOODH*

- Soak ½ cup / 75 gm almonds (*badam*) in plenty of water for 8 hours.

- Peel, blend with 2½ cups / 500 ml water and combine until it has a smooth textue.

- Sieve through a muslin cloth or a fine strainer and refrigerate. Stir and use as per recipe requirement.

TIP
- Consume within 3 days.
- To remove the skin easily, you can soak the almonds in slightly hot water for 8 hours.

IDLI BATTER

1

- Wash and soak de-husked, split black lentil (*dhuli urad dal*) in plenty of water for 8 hours.

2

- Wash and soak 1 cup / 200 gms boiled rice, 1 cup / 200 gms raw rice and ½ tsp fenugreek seeds (*methi dana*) in plenty of water for 10 hours.

3

- Drain the water of rice and lentil (*dal*). Blend in a food processor together with water to medium-thick consistency with a slightly coarse texture. Remove.

4

- Add 1 tsp salt and leave it to ferment at room temperature for 10–12 hours.

5

- Use as per the recipe requirement.

TIP
- In summer, the batter takes 12 hours to ferment, and in winters it may take 1–2 days.
- After fermentation, refrigerate the batter and consume within 3–4 days.

DIABETES MEAL PLAN

	BREAKFAST	LUNCH	SNACK	DINNER
MONDAY	Lentil Pancakes (*Dal Aur Methi Ka Chilla*) Green Gooseberry Chutney (*Hari Amla Chutney*) Tangy Date Chutney (*Khajoor Ki Saunth*)	Nutty Spinach Salad (*Thandi Palak Salaad*) Whole Red Lentil with Goosefoot Leaves (*Bathua Aur Kale Masoor Ki Dal*) Water Chestnut and Mushroom (*Singhara Aur Khumb*) Black Gram Flour Bread (*Kaale Chane Ki Roti*)	Pure & Simple ABC Juice (*Seeda Sada ABC Juice*) Fenugreek Savoury Cake (*Methi Muthia*) Green Gooseberry Chutney (*Hari Amla Chutney*)	Evergreen Soup (*Harabhara Shorba*) Gravy-Style Indian Baby Pumpkin (*Rassedar Tinda*) Rice Lentil Hotchpotch (*Sabjiyon Ki Khichdi*) Mixed Vegetable Yoghurt (*Pachdi Raita*)
TUESDAY / SATURDAY	Barnyard Millet Feast (*Samvat Upma*)	Lotus Stem & Zucchini Salad (*Kamal Kakdi Aur Zucchini Salaad*) Lentil Stew (*Sambhar*) Bitter Gourd with Spring Onions (*Hara Pyaz Ka Karela*) Red Rice Pilaf (*Kerala Pulao*)	Lemongrass Tea (*Nimbu Ghans Chai*) Zesty Lotus Stem Treat (*Kamal Kakdi Ki Chaat*)	Baby Bok Choy & Onion Soup (*Pattidar Shorba*) Bottle Gourd & Green Gram Lentil (*Lauki Aur Moong Ki Dal*) Carrots with Fenugreek Leaves (*Gajar Methi*) Spicy Vegetable Pilaf (*Subz Biryani*)
WEDNESDAY	Pearl Millet Pancakes (*Bajra Uttapam*) Fresh Mint Yoghurt (*Pudina Raita*)	Water Chestnut Salad (*Singhara Khira Salaad*) Fenugreek-Flavoured Yellow Lentil (*Arhar Daal Aur Methi*) Cluster Beans with Fenugreek Sprouts (*Guar Phali Aur Methi*) Sorghum Flat Bread (*Jowar Roti*)	Digestive Tea (*Ayurvedic Chai*) Lentil Pancakes (*Dal Aur Methi Ka Chilla*) Green Gooseberry Chutney (*Hari Amla Chutney*)	Baby Bok Choy & Onion Soup (*Pattidar Shorba*) Gravy Button Mushroom (*Rasedar Khumb*) Ginger-Flavoured Cauliflower (*Adraki Gobhi*) Zucchini & Broccoli Pilaf (*Zucchini & Broccoli Ka Pulao*)
THURSDAY / SUNDAY	Savoury Flattened Red Rice (*Lal Poha*)	Mixed Green Gram Salad (*Kosambari*) Gravy-Style Indian Baby Pumpkin (*Rassedar Tinda*) Dry Colocasia (*Sookhi Arvi*) Rice Bread (*Chawal Ki Roti*)	Flavoured Butter Milk (*Chaas*) Roasted Feast (*Farsan*)	Broccoli Soup (*Hari Phoolgobi Ka Shorba*) Bottle Gourd Dumplings in Yoghurt Gravy (*Lauki Kofta Kadhi*) Ridged Gourd Rice (*Turai Ke Chawal*)
FRIDAY	Mixed Lentil Pancake (*Adai Dosa*) Tomato Relish (*Tamatar Ki Chutney*)	Tricolour Salad (*Tirangi Cholia Salaad*) Mix Vegetable Curry (*Sindhi Kadhi*) Coastal Red Amaranth (*Lal Saag*) Barnyard Millet with Bottle Gourd (*Samak Ke Chawal*)	Summer Cooler (*Mast Mast Sherbet*) Tangy Bean Sprouts (*Chatpati Ankurit Moong*)	Split Green Gram Soup (*Moong Daal Shorba*) Spicy Vegetable Pilaf (*Subz Biryani*) Spinach Yoghurt (*Palak Raita*)

GENERAL WELLBEING MEAL PLAN

BREAKFAST	LUNCH	SNACK	DINNER	
Barnyard Millet Feast (*Samvat Upma*) Lemongrass Tea (*Nimbu Ghans Chai*)	Watermelon Salad (*Tarbooz Ka Salaad*) Spicy Vegetable Pilaf (*Subz Biryani*) Mix Vegetable Curry (*Sindhi Kadhi*) Stuffed Pointed Gourd (*Bharwa Parwal*)	Tangy Mint Lemonade (*Zaikedaar Shikanji*) Tea Time Treat (*Chana Murmura*)	Maize & Spring Onion Bread (*Makka Aur Hara Pyaz Ka Paratha*) Whole Red Lentil with Goosefoot Leaves (*Bathua Aur Kale Masoor Ki Daal*) Carrot Delight (*Gajar Ki Kheer*)	MONDAY
Quinoa Porridge (*Quinoa Daliya*)	Black Rice & Avocado Salad (*Chawal Ki Tirangi Salaad*) Mixed Millet Bread (*Mishrit Anaaj Ki Roti*) Bitter Gourd with Spring Onions (*Hara Pyaz Ka Karela*) Carrots with Fenugreek Leaves (*Gajar Methi*)	Pure & Simple ABC Juice (*Seeda Sada ABC Juice*) Roasted Feast (*Farsan*)	Spicy Lentil Rice (*Bisi Bele Bhaath*) Tangy Turmeric Root (*Khatti Kachchi Haldi*) Finger Millet Bites (*Ragi Meeng Paag*)	TUESDAY / SATURDAY
Pearl Millet Pancakes (*Bajra Uttapam*) Fresh Mint Yoghurt (*Pudina Raita*)	Sorghum Flat Bread (*Jowar Roti*) Coastal Red Amaranth (*Lal Saag*) Bottle Gourd Dumplings in Yoghurt Gravy (*Lauki Kofta Kadhi*)	Nutty Banana Cooler (*Badami Banana Thandai*)	Zucchini & Broccoli Pilaf (*Zucchini Aur Broccoli Ka Pulao*) Fenugreek-Flavoured Yellow Lentil (*Arhar Daal Aur Methi*) Palm Jaggery Rice (*Gud Ke Chawal*)	WEDNESDAY
Savoury Flattened Red Rice (*Lal Poha*)	Roasted Pumpkin Salad (*Bhuna Kaddu Ka Mila-jula Salaad*) Lacy Rice Pancake (*Chawal Ka Dosa*) Green Plantain Vegetable (*Kache Kele Ki Sabji*) Lentil Stew (*Sambhar*)	Papaya-Coco Shake (*Papita-Nariyal Sherbet*) Zesty Lotus Stem Treat (*Kamal Kakdi Ki Chaat*)	Sorghum & Lentil Fusion (*Jowar Khichdi*) Star Fruit Delight (*Kamrak Ki Launji*) Jaggery-Coated Sweet Potato (*Meethi Shakarkandi*)	THURSDAY / SUNDAY
Finger Millet Pancake (*Ragi Dosa*) Lentil Stew (*Sambhar*)	Nutty Spinach Salad (*Thandi Palak Salaad*) Zucchini & Broccoli Pilaf (*Zucchini Aur Broccoli Ka Pulao*) Gravy Button Mushroom (*Rasedar Khumb*)	Summer Cooler (*Mast Mast Sherbet*) Fenugreek Savoury Cake (*Methi Muthia*)	Crispy Rice Bread (*Akki Roti*) Gravy-Style Indian Baby Pumpkin (*Rassedar Tinda*) Barnyard Millet Mango Pudding (*Samak Aur Aam Ki Kheer*)	FRIDAY

HEART DISEASE MEAL PLAN

	BREAKFAST	LUNCH	SNACK	DINNER
MONDAY	Finger Millet Rice Cake (*Ragi Idli*) Roasted Peanut Chutney (*Moongphalli Ki Chutney*)	Nutty Spinach Salad (*Thandi Palak Salaad*) Butter Beans in Tomato Gravy (*Taridar Vaal Ki Sabji*) Cluster Beans with Fenugreek Sprouts (*Guar Phali Aur Methi*) Mixed Millet Bread (*Mishrit Anaaj Ki Roti*)	Flavoured Butter Milk (*Chaas*) Tangy Bean Sprouts (*Chatpati Ankurit Moong*)	Broccoli Soup (*Hari Phoolgobi Ka Shorba*) Lentil Stew (*Sambhar*) Carrots & Flat Green Beans (*Gajar Aur Sem Phali*) Red Rice Pilaf (*Kerala Pulao*)
TUESDAY / SATURDAY	Savoury Flattened Red Rice (*Lal Poha*)	Beetroot Salad (*Chukandar Ka Salaad*) Garlic-Flavoured Spinach (*Lehsuni Palak*) Bottle Gourd & Green Gram Lentil (*Lauki Aur Moong Ki Dal*) Black Gram Flour Bread (*Kaale Chane Ki Roti*)	Savoury Lentil Cakes (*Moong Dal Dhokla*) Digestive Tea (*Ayurvedic Chai*)	Spiced Pumpkin Soup (*Kaddu Ka Shorba*) Fenugreek-Flavoured Yellow Lentil (*Arhar Daal Aur Methi*) Zucchini & Broccoli Pilaf (*Zucchini Aur Broccoli Ka Pulao*)
WEDNESDAY	Buckwheat Pancakes (*Kuttu Ka Cheela*) Yoghurt – Non-flavoured, low-fat (*Dahi*)	Watermelon Salad (*Tarbooz Ka Salaad*) Ginger-Flavoured Cauliflower (*Adraki Gobhi*) Curried Black-eyed Peas (*Rassedar Lobia*) Maize & Spring Onion Bread (*Makka Aur Hara Pyaz Ka Paratha*)	Tangy Mint Lemonade (*Zaikedaar Shikanji*) Roasted Feast (*Farsan*)	Garden Soup (*Sabz Shorba*) Spicy Vegetable Pilaf (*Subz Biryani*) Bottle Gourd Dumplings in Yoghurt Gravy (*Lauki Kofta kadhi*)
THURSDAY / SUNDAY	Quinoa Porridge (*Quinoa Daliya*)	Roasted Pumpkin Salad (*Bhuna Kaddu Ka Mila-jula Salaad*) Lentil Stew (*Sambhar*) Carrots & Flat Green Beans (*Gajar Aur Sem Phali*) Crispy Rice Bread (*Akki Roti*)	Flavoured Butter Milk (*Chaas*) Sprouted Black Chickpea Delicacy (*Ankurit Chana Chaat*)	Button Mushroom Soup (*Khumb Shorba*) Butter Beans in Tomato Gravy (*Taridar Vaal Ki Sabji*) Barnyard Millet with Bottle Gourd (*Samak Ke Chawal*)
FRIDAY	Mixed Lentil Pancake (*Adai Dosa*) Tomato Relish (*Tamatar Ki Chutney*)	Garden Salad (*Hari Bhari Salaad*) Gravy-Style Indian Baby Pumpkin (*Rassedar Tinda*) Sorghum Flat Bread (*Jowar Roti*) Fenugreek-Flavoured Yellow Lentil (*Arhar Daal Aur Methi*)	Roasted Rice Cake (*Paniharan*) Yoghurt-Mustard Sauce (*Sarson Chutney*)	Black Chickpea Soup (*Kale Chane Ka Shorba*) Garlic-Flavoured Spinach (*Lehsuni Palak*) Dry Colocasia (*Sookhi Arvi*) Rice Lentil Hotchpotch (*Sabjiyon Ki Khichdi*)

HYPOTHYROID MEAL PLAN

	BREAKFAST	LUNCH	SNACK	DINNER	
	Mixed Lentil Pancake (*Adai Dosa*) PP Tomato Relish (*Tamatar Ki Chutney*)	Lotus Stem & Zucchini Salad (*Kamal Kakdi Aur Zucchini Salaad*) Ridged Gourd Rice (*Turai Ke Chawal*) Bottle Gourd Dumplings in Yoghurt Gravy (*Lauki Kofta Kadhi*) Bitter Gourd with Spring Onions (*Hara Pyaz Ka Karela*)	Tender Coconut Breezer (*Harayali Daab Sherbet*) Zesty Lotus Stem Treat (*Kamal Kakdi Ki Chaat*)	Button Mushroom Soup (*Khumb Shorba*) Mixed Vegetable Quinoa (*Sabz Quinoa*)	MONDAY
	Roasted Rice Cake (*Paniharan*) Lentil Stew (*Sambhar*)	Crispy Rice Bread (*Akki Roti*) Stuffed Pointed Gourd (*Bharwa Parwal*) Butter Beans in Tomato Gravy (*Taridar Vaal Ki Sabji*)	Tangy Mint Lemonade (*Zaikedaar Shikanji*) Tangy Bean Sprouts (*Chatpati Ankurit Moong*)	Black Chickpea Soup (*Kale Chane Ka Shorba*) Spicy Lentil Rice (*Bisi Bele Bhaath*) Mixed Vegetable Yoghurt (*Pachdi Raita*)	TUESDAY / SATURDAY
	Savoury Flattened Red Rice (*Lal Poha*) Papaya-Coco Shake (*Papita-Nariyal Sherbet*)	Tricolour Salad (*Tirangi Cholia Salaad*) Mixed Vegetable Quinoa (*Sabz Quinoa*) Mix Vegetable Curry (*Sindhi Kadhi*)	Digestive Tea (*Ayurvedic Chai*) Green Banana Cutlets (*Kache Kele Ki Tikki*)	Baby Bok Choy & Onion Soup (*Pattidar Shorba*) Crispy Rice Bread (*Akki Roti*) Bottle Gourd Dumplings in Yoghurt Gravy (*Lauki Kofta Kadhi*)	WEDNESDAY
	Mixed Lentil Pancake (*Adai Dosa*) Tomato Relish (*Tamatar Ki Chutney*)	Water Chestnut Salad (*Singhara Khira Salaad*) Black Gram Flour Bread (*Kaale Chane Ki Roti*) Carrots & Flat Green Beans (*Gajar Aur Sem Phali*) Bottle Gourd & Green Gram Lentil (*Lauki Aur Moong Ki Dal*)	Lemongrass Tea (*Nimbu Ghans Chai*) Rice Noodles with Bean Sprouts (*Chawal Ki Sewai Aur Ankurit Moong*)	Roasted Bell Pepper Soup (*Bhuni Shimla Mirch Ka Shorba*) Ridged Gourd Rice (*Turai Ke Chawal*) Fenugreek-Flavoured Yellow Lentil (*Arhar Daal Aur Methi*)	THURSDAY / SUNDAY
	Savoury Lentil Cakes (*Moong Dal Dhokla*) Green Gooseberry Chutney (*Hari Amla Chutney*)	Spicy Vegetable Pilaf (*Subz Biryani*) Mixed Vegetable Yoghurt (*Pachdi Raita*)	Flavoured Butter Milk (*Chaas*) Roasted Feast (*Farsan*)	Spiced Pumpkin Soup (*Kaddu Ka Shorba*) Ridged Gourd Rice (*Turai Ke Chawal*) Butter Beans in Tomato Gravy (*Taridar Vaal Ki Sabji*)	FRIDAY

INDEX